Let Mercy Abound

Let Mercy Abound

Social Concern in the Greek Orthodox Church

By

Stanley Samuel Harakas

Let us make mercy abundant, let us give proof of much love to man, both by the use of our money, and by our actions. And if we see any one ill-treated and beaten in the market-place, whether we can pay down money, let us do it: or whether by words we may separate them, let us not be backward. For even a word has its reward.

Saint John Chrysostomos
Homily 15, The Sermon on the Mount

Holy Cross Orthodox Press
Brookline, Massachusetts 02146
1983

Published by Holy Cross Orthodox Press
Brookline, Massachusetts 02146

Cover design by Mary C. Vaporis

Financial assistance toward the publication
of this book has also been received from the
Taylor Foundation.

Library of Congress Cataloging in Publication Data

Harakas, Stanley S.
  Let mercy abound.

  Includes bibliographical references and index.
    1. Church and social problems—Greek Orthodox
Archdiocese of North and South America. 2. Greek
Orthodox Archdiocese of North and South America—
Doctrines. 3. Orthodox Eastern Church—United States.
I. Title.
HN39.U6H37 1983   261.8'3   83-18602
ISBN 0-916586-60-X
ISBN 0-916586-61-8 (pbk.)

Dedication

"To the only wise God be glory for evermore though Jesus Christ"

Romans 16.27

and

Archbishop Iakovos, whose leadership in social concern
made this book possible

CONTENTS

INTRODUCTION

This book is a chronicle of statements, events, and teachings which bring to light a little-known and little-appreciated aspect of the life of the Eastern Orthodox Church-social concern as an aspect of the life and thought of this ancient, "Mother Church" of the Christian tradition.

More specifically, it documents a series of three separate but closely related phenomena, which when held together and examined closely, reveal a pattern of development of great interest for those concerned with the witness of the Church in the world today.

The period of time covered in this chronicle is short—a little over twenty years, coinciding with the hierarchical service of Archbishop Iakovos (Coucouzis) as Primate of the Greek Orthodox Archdiocese of North and South America, 1958-1980. But more than this, it is a chronicle of the rapid change in the outlook and orientation of an Orthodox Church which arrived on these shores from Europe in a wave of immigration at the turn of the century.

On the one hand, this book is the description of the impact of the thoughts, concerns and visions of Archbishop Iakovos upon the social consciousness of his church. On the other, it is a chronicle of the interplay between a charismatic and visionary church leader and the Christian conscience of the lay and clergy leadership of the Greek Orthodox Church in the Americas. It is also a chronicle which describes the reawakening of the long-dormant tradition of Eastern Orthodox social consiciousness and concern.

The first chapter seeks to describe, on the basis of recent studies, the tradition of social concern in early Greek Christianity, the Byzantine period, the five-hundred year period of Turkish domination of much of Eastern Orthodoxy, and some modern efforts for the development of social concern in Greece. It also seeks to briefly describe the attitude of Greek Orthodox Christians in North America prior to 1958, when Archbishop Iakovos assumed the spiritual leadership of the 1,000,000 member Greek Orthodox Archdiocese of North and South America.

This is followed by a presentation of the elements of social concern to be found in the encyclicals of Archbishop Iakovos over the twenty year period under discussion. An examination of the social concerns content of the keynote addresses given by the Archbishop at the Biennial Clergy-Laity Congresses follows. The next chapter is an account of the decisions of the Social and Moral Issues Committees of the Clergy-Laity Congresses of the Greek Orthodox Archdiocese of North and South America, together with some additional relevant material. As part of the documentary character of this book, Chapter Five presents the official texts of the Social and Moral Issues Committees of the Clergy-Laity Congresses. A final chapter attempts some conclusions, delineates some problems which need further study, and outlines possible future courses of action.

Special thanks are due to His Eminence Archbishop Iakovos who granted permission for access to the Archdiocesan files. Also, I wish to express thanks to my colleague, Father Demetrios J. Constantelos, who edited the encyclicals of the Greek Orthodox Archdiocese dealing with Orthodox Christian philanthropy and social concern upon which much of chapter two is based. Further, I wish to express thanks to the Director of Communications of the Archdiocese, Father Alexander Karloustos whose encouragement was most valuable in making the decision to proceed with the completion of this study, and to Father Nomikos Michael Vaporis, Director of Holy Cross Orthodox Press, who encouraged its publication and saw it through from its earliest forms to the present.

To Cathy Lazarides, Pauline Pavlakos, and my dear wife, Emily, who were responsbile for typing and retyping the manuscript through various stages of its preparation, I express heartfelt thanks.

Special thanks and appreciation are due to Mr. Andrew A. Athens, National Chairman of the United Hellenic American Congress, and to Mr. Alex Gianaras, Mr. Chris Kritikos, and Mr. George Christopher, all of Chicago, for their financial support which made possible the publication of this study.

In conclusion, I wish to express special gratitude to those students who throughout the years have shown interest and Christian enthusiasm for the Orthodox witness in the contemporary world. It is they who contributed, and continue to do so, to my own commitment and the need for Orthodox Christians to articulate and live the social implications of the Orthodox Christian Faith in this age and this place. May this humble offering respond to their enthusiasm and serious concern.

S. S. Harakas
Feast of the Holy Unmercenaries
Kosmas and Damianos

Chapter One

THE TRADITION OF SOCIAL CONCERN
IN THE ORTHODOX CHURCH

Two Sundays before the beginning of the Great Lent, the lection-
ary of the Orthodox Church requires the reading of the account of
the Last Judgment as recorded in the 25th chapter of the Gospel
according to St. Matthew. It is a vivid account which focuses upon
works of philanthropy and acts of concern for the welfare of fellow
human beings who are in need: feeding the hungry, giving water to
the thirsty, clothing the naked, comforting the sick, visiting the imprisoned. The chief theme of the hymns appointed for the day is
the judgment itself and the need for the believer to repent and prepare for it. But the related requirement for philanthropy and social
concern by the worshipers is far from absent. Thus, one of the
hymns of the day says:

> Knowing the commands of the Lord, let us live out our lives in
> this way: let us give nourishment to those who hunger, let us give
> drink to those who thirst, let us cover those who are naked, let
> us gather in to us those who are strangers, and, those who are
> sick and imprisoned let us visit, so that he who will in the future
> judge the whole earth, may say to us as well, 'Come, you blessed
> ones of my Father, and inherit the Kingdom which has been
> prepared for you.'[1]

The teaching of Jesus, which highlighted love as the chief virtue,
led effortlessly to the concern for the welfare of others. Philanthropy for those who suffered became an expression of genuine
Christian life. Thus, St. Paul conducted a drive during his missionary travels to help the poor in Jerusalem.[2]

Numerous studies have shown this dimension of Christian concern for the welfare of others in the teaching of Jesus Christ and
the New Testament Church.[3] This concern, on the one hand, is an
outgrowth of the Christian faith itself. On the other, it is an outgrowth of the Christian reaction to the non-Christian social realities with which it had to contend. Thus, it is possible to trace out
in some detail the attitudes of Jesus Christ toward ethical questions
in general, as well as Jesus' teaching and attitudes toward the state,
war, the family, and property.[4] The same can be seen in the New
Testament Church.[5]

The rapid growth of the Church during the first three centuries raised many issues of social concern, though these were not at the center of its activities as it sought to secure its presence in the Roman Empire. Some, however, hold that it was precisely the ethical and moral life-style, including philanthropy and concern for the welfare of the poor, the suffering and the dispossessed which attracted the attention of persons destined to become new believers in the Christian Church, rather than overt missionary efforts. [6] The Christian life could not be understood, for example, without concern for the poor, for slaves, for the protection of children both born and unborn, for the release of captives, etc. There was a special problem for the early persecuted Church. It was how to make sense out of the delay of Christ's expected return and the day-to-day obligations of life and the Christian love which it required. The tension for the Christian was further intensified by the intermittent persecutions. The Apologists of the Church, that band of Christian writers who took up the defense of the Church before her literary and political enemies, however, never failed to deal with questions of ethics and public morality. It is not difficult to document this continuing social and philanthropic concern. [7]

The flowering of Christian social concern and philanthropy came into being with the legalization and subsequent establishment of the Church in the Christianized Roman Empire, which came to be known as Byzantium. Thus, it becomes possible to trace the history of Christian concern with the Pagan state, the Christian state, the family, education, property, philanthropy, slavery, and public spectacles. [8] This concern also expressed itself in practical organizational fashion as well with church and monastically supported and administered institutions such as hospitals, hospices, homes for the aged, orphanages, houses for the poor, reformatory houses, cemeteries for strangers and home for the blind. [9]

This Christian concern embodied itself in the consciousness of the state, and particularly in the person of the emperor. The emperor was never conceived of as a purely secular ruler. Whenever reflection was made, or advice given to the emperor about his duties and role, the concern for the well-being of the subjects, cast in terms of Christ-like philanthropy was always made. Thus Agapetos wrote "An Exposition of Heads of Advice and Counsel" addressing it to Emperor Justinian I around the year 530. Counseling the emperor he said that he "becomes worthy of God, when he does nothing unworthy of Him, but thinks things that are God's, speaks what He thinks, and does what He speaks . . . Nothing gives a man such good repute as to be able to do what He wills, and to will and do acts of kindness (in Greek, *Philanthropia*) . . . Therefore, since God of His grace has given you the power which your good will towards us needed for our sake, may you both will and do things as please Him Who gave you this power."[10]

Particularly, some Church Fathers were concerned with issues of philanthropy and social concern. Thus, the efforts of St. Basil, who spoke and taught extensively regarding concern for the down-trodden, the poor, the unjustly used, as well as issues such as the relation of the Christian faith to culture, the state, and family issues has been well documented.[11] His establishment of the famed 'Basilias' outside Caesarea of Asia Minor as a multi-faceted agency of social concern and welfare is well known. Even better known for his social concern is St. John Chrysostom, whose perceptive mind was closely attuned to the social realities of his time. Thus, his modern day biographer says that "one may call Chrysostom without exaggeration the most significant moralist and ethical preacher of his time." And as a result of his immense productivity and popularity, "he has also become, for following centuries, the most distinguished moral teacher of his people."[12] He was particularly sensitive to the responsibility of the rich for the poor, and would broach no excuses from the rich in their denial of the needs of the poor while they lived in superfluous luxury. Witness these passages revealing a sharp and clear social conscience from Chrysostom's preaching.

It is foolishness and public madness to fill the cupboards with clothing, and allow men who are created in God's image and and our likeness, to stand naked and trembling with the cold, so that they can hardly hold themselves upright. Yes, you say, he is cheating, and is only pretending to be weak and trembling. What! Do you not fear that lightning from heaven will fall on you for this word? Only see, you are large and fat, you hold drinking parties until late at night, and sleep in warm soft bed, and do you not think of how you must give an account of your misuse of the gifts of God?

You question very closely the poor and the miserable, who are scarcely better off in this respect than the dead; you do not fear the dreadful and terrible judgment seat of Christ. If the beggar lies, he lies from necessity, because your hard-heartedness and merciless inhumanity force him to such cheating. For who would otherwise be so wretched and pitiful that he would needlessly, for the sake of a little bread, so demean himself as to let himself be struck and mishandled? If we would give our alms gladly and willingly, the poor would never have fallen to such depths. And what shall I say of nakedness and cold? I will tell you of some terrible cases. It has happened that people in need have blinded their own children at an early age in order to conquer our heartlessness. Because neither their youth nor their misery was able to awaken the hard hearted, even though while being naked, they could still see, therefore they added on a still greater misfortune in order to quiet their hunger. They thought it would be easier even to bear blindness than to battle with perpetual hunger and die a most miserable death. And there are also other people... who, if their begging accomplishes nothing, begin to do tricks, by which they surpass the best buffoons and magicians. Some eat the leather from old shoes, some drive sharp nails into their heads, others sit with their bare bodies in freezing water or do other foolish things in order to present a ridiculous spectacle. And you stand by, laughing and staring, and entertaining yourself with his strange misery, while the human nature, common to us all is dishonored. And in order that he may perform his tricks better, you give him money.

But for him who prays and calls on God, who beseeches you humbly and modestly, to him you will vouchsafe neither an answer or a glance, but at the most, you will give him a reproach. and say: Why does such a one have to live and breathe and see the light of the sun? And while God says to you: Give alms, and I will give thee the kingdom of heaven, you hear not: but if the devil shows you a head with nails sticking in it, then you become very generous! And still you ask why there is a hell? Ask rather, why there is only *one*![13]

As a preacher, teacher, and through personal example, Chrysostom's incisive and thoroughly formed social conscience has a continuing effect on the life and thought of Orthodox people.[14] As a patristic authority, his teaching on moral and social issues continues to provide a pattern and model for those who would concern themselves with these issues from the Eastern Orthodox perspective.[15]

With the fall of the Byzantine Empire in the fifteenth century, a situation developed which severely limited social concern and outreach as well as thought about it expressed in written documents. The whole Church was placed in a survival stance. The Mohammedan overlords established an Islamic theocracy in which Christians could exist merely as a tolerated minority under severe limitations, exploitation and restrictions. The new situation demanded a restricted character of life for the Orthodox under the domination of the Ottomans. Though the Patriarch was granted extensive jurisdiction over the Christian population of the new empire, the daily life of the Christian population was hardly more than a tolerated existence. The Orthodox Christians were not ever permitted to forget their subject status. No churches could be built without official approval, which was granted sparingly. Even the repair of a church required official permission. Christians were forced to wear distinctive clothing. None but the Patriarch was permitted to ride on horseback. Officially prohibited from service in the armed forces, they were forced sometimes to do the menial tasks in the naval service. "Christian families had to submit to arbitrary seizure of their young sons, to be converted to Islam and enrolled in the Janissary regiments."[16] Pressure was put on Christians to convert to Islam, but if a Mohammedan converted to Christianity, he was subject to death according to Islamic law. And if a Christian who had converted to Islam, even under coercion, repented and returned to his prior Christian faith, he was liable to be put to death. Law suits between Christian and Muslims had to be heard in Muslim courts "and few Muslim judges were prepared to give a judgment in favor of the unbeliever."[17]

Survival became the watchword. Even the few privileges granted to the conquered Christians "were more effective on paper than in fact. The Turks could not forget that they were the ruling race, the conquerors of the Christians and it irked them that the Greeks should retain privileges that no conquered infidel race ought to enjoy." The following seventeenth century account of the state of Christian life is helpful for the reader to understand the situation:

Sir Paul Ricaut, an Englishman of Spanish descent, who had travelled widely in the East, wrote at the request of King Charles II a book entitled *The Present State of the Greek and Armenian Churches, Anno Christi 1678*. In it he states that the election to the Patriarchate was vested "rather in the hands of the Turks than of the bishops." He was deeply moved by the position of the Greeks.

Tragically [he writes] the subversion of the Sanctuaries of Religion, the Royal Priesthood expelled from their Churches, and these converted into Mosques; the Mysteries of the altar concealed in secret and dark places; for such I have seen in Cities and Villages where I have travelled, rather like Vaults and Sepulchres than Churches, having their roofs almost levelled with the Superficies of the Earth, lest the most ordinary Exurgency of Structure should be accused for Triumph of Religion, and stand in competition with the lofty spire of the Mahometan Mosque.

Ricaut understood well the difficulties that faced the Greek Church. Indeed, knowing what he did, he was amazed that it had survived at all.

It is no wonder [he wrote] to human reason that considers the Oppression and the Contempt that good Christians are exposed to, and the Ignorance in their Churches occasioned through Poverty in the Clergy, that many should be found who retreat from the Faith; but it is, rather a Miracle, and a true Verification of those Words of Christ, that the Gates of Hell shall not be able to prevail against his Church, that there is conserved still amongst so much Opposition, and in spite of all Tyranny and Arts contrived against it, an open and public Profession of the Christian Faith.[19]

The result of this condition was that, outside of a small aristocracy, learning barely survived, poverty reigned, and life— though continued—was precarious. The fickle whims of the Moslem overlord created a new class of saints—the neomartyrs, who were simple common folk who when provoked would refuse to deny their faith. They would frequently suffer fearsome torturous deaths as a result.[20]

Yet the people, their clergy, and the Church survived. In such a humiliated condition there could be no thought of mission, no thought of social structures which were totally out of the sphere of influence of the Christians, and no possiblity for any outreach. Yet, even under these depressing circumstances, efforts were made to care for the most abused, miserable, and suffering. A historian of Christian missions, in describing Orthodox mission styles, evaluates them in the following revealing judgment:

The Greek Church . . . does not covet power. It would rather dispense gifts than govern. And how many gifts it has given! The holy rites it offers to the convert embrace his entire life. There is no important event from birth to death which it is not ready to consecrate, no emergency in private or public life for which it has no comfort. It appeared everywhere as a kind helper in the weariness of life, and thus won all hearts.

Such was its attitude as well during this difficult period in its life which lasted for about 500 years, one quarter of its historical existence! Yet, the Church did not confine its 'gifts' to the liturgical sphere alone. The Church assumed, with its limited resources, the stance of a protective and caring parent. Besides the poor boxes, it established traditions, customs and practices which encouraged practical concern for its own poor

and suffering. It penetrated its own local parish life, trade organizations and other groups with the philanthropic spirit. Institutions were established through major gifts from emigrant co-
religionists and fellow-Greeks. Of special attention were children
and young people. The giving of dowries to poor girls so that—
in accordance with the customs of the day—they could marry,
and the care of orphans, are examples of this care. Nor were
those who justly or—not infrequently—unjustly were imprisoned
ignored by the Christian conscience. Hospitals were established
and supported.[22] Such concern was primarily expressed by
individuals (hierarchs, lower clergy, and laity) because of the
serious restrictions of the situation. A few became personages
of widespread fame within the captive people. Such a one was
a priest by the name of Kosmas Aitolos, dubbed 'The Apostle
of the Poor,' who lived in Greece during the eighteenth century. From 1760 to 1779 he was an itinerant preacher. "In addition to feeding the soul, Father Kosmas attempted to feed the
body as well as the mind. He spoke out against social injustices,
against the abuse of the poor and uneducated and against the
inequities that existed between men and women."[23] He was
particularly interested in education on the primary level, which
meant concern with illiteracy. "Father Kosmas was persuasive
enough so that in over two hundred towns and villages he was
instrumental in establishing schools where none existed before.
His moral authority was such that he was able, not only to raise
money needed to establish the schools and to maintain them, but,
with the consent of the inhabitants, to appoint teachers and
overseers for those schools, as illustrated from his letters."[24]

Yet these were rare lighthouses in a dark and stormy sea.
The natural concern with survival, with protection from the
hostile political, social, and religious environment, not only did
not permit a concern with issues of social concern, but also
severely restricted the possibility of thoughtful treatment of such
topics.

Nor did the situation change much after the Turkish yoke
began, little by little, to be removed from the Orthodox peoples.
The first successful revolution began in 1821. At the turn of
the next decade, a small portion of Greece was free, yet subject
to a poverty-limited existence. Many years would go by before
full freedom from the Ottoman Empire would become a reality.
Of importance for what is to follow below regarding the social
attitudes of the Greek Orthodox in this country, many Greek

Orthodox immigrants emigrated to find their fortunes (1890-1920) not only from free Greece, but from areas still under the control of the Ottoman Empire. [25] Not surprisingly, the 'survival mentality' was reinforced by residence in a strange land. Yet, as the years went by, a social consciousness began to be restored. Concern with some of these issues even began to re-enter the spheres of interest of the theological thought of the time.

Thus, a remarkable breadth of interest for social problems was evinced, surprisingly, in an Orthodox Christian ethics handbook published in Constantinople in 1927, by Vasileios Antoniades. In addition to the theoretical questions and the traditional general material on personal ethics, as well as the social institutions of family, state, and church, Antoniades addressed a wide range of then (and still) current social issues: personal freedom, health and health services, death, euthanasia, war and peace movements, hunger, feminism, social and economic justice, scientific and technological progress, equal justice, law and order, marriage and divorce, Church and modern nation-state, etc. [26] There is to be noted in the treatment of these topics an open, informed and contemporary attitude which seeks to honestly deal with varying and often contradictory views. This breadth seems to be missing from a contemporary work, long considered standard, published in Greece itself. [27]

In particular, the scene on the North American continent tended to reflect the attitudes in the second of the above mentioned books, rather than the first. North America, in particular, became one of the chief areas sought as a place of opportunity by the increasing tide of emigrant Orthodox.

These peoples were large enough in numbers to form a "diaspora," a community of like-minded people who maintained an ecclesiastical and ethnic identity with their homelands and traditions, but concurrently, a much too small minority to assume a sense of responsibility and concern for the public welfare. Among the Greeks, there seems to have been another factor at work as well. Sociological studies of the Greek-American mentality have noted an "initial predisposition toward individualism." Beyond the strong "love and discipline that are the family's real glue," for the Greek Orthodox immigrant, "individual striving was considered more important than group betterment." Significantly, "Greek Americans have preferred to present a face of decorum in their relations with the general public and in their dealings with political leaders," [28] but very little involvement of a substantive character.

As far as the national Greek Orthodox Church was concerned, its almost exclusive concern focused upon questions of the organizational 'nightmare' of conflicting parties. In 1931 Archbishop Athenagoras (Spyrou) assumed the task of bringing order and unity out of chaos. When he left in 1949 to assume the Patriarchal Throne of Constantinople, he left a small, but essentially united and organized ecclesial body. Nearly all his efforts were inward oriented. "The face of decorum," was, of course, present always in dealing with the American social realities, but there was little engagement and little sense of ecclesial responsibility for the social and moral problems of the society in which the Greek-American existed. Efforts were made to recognize a connection and relationship to the hospitality and freedom offered them in the Americas and a duty was recognized "to participate in everything that regards the national American soul."[29] In practice, however, the concern focused around celebrations and observances, the American war effort and the effect of World War II on Greece. In the collected encyclicals of Archbishop Athenagoras, forty-six of them are designated as ethnic or socially oriented.[30] Seven of these are generally celebratory in character, (e.g., Washington's Birthday, Brotherhood Day, the World's Fair, etc.). Ten of them are clearly philanthropic: (1) Near East Relief, (6) American Red Cross, (2) Greek Orphans, (1) Ecumenical Patriarchate. Ten deal with the war effort primarily from an American perspective: (3) General, (4) War Bonds, (1) Pearl Harbor, (1) Russian Hospital Aid, (1) War Victory. The balance are related to Greece, and the Greek aspect of the War: (1) Liturgical mention of Greek King, Greek Independence Day (each year), (4) 28 October, (1) Capture of Crete, (1) Bulgarian Mass execution of 15,000 Greeks, (9) Greek War Relief, (1) "Adopt a Greek City Postwar Campaign," (1) Justice For Greece Committee, totalling 19 encyclicals. Of all, one could be called clearly socially oriented in terms of American social structures—an encyclical on labor and management relations as embodied in the National Relief Act (N.R.A.). It is clear that the Church was being co-opted by outside agencies, but was assuming hardly any initiative on its own for social issues. Perhaps one can justify this because of the all-consuming demands of the war effort. On the other hand, it seems reasonable to assume that the major concerns of the Church were not at all ready for outward involvement. Philanthropy, in responding to disasters—primarily in Greece—was conducted, but the inner organization of the Archdiocese was the major focus of Athenagoras' hierarchical service. However, he did manage to turn the face of the

Church outward as well. His personality related well with those in power and authority in the nation. "He managed to become the respected friend of presidents, governors and senators. Wherever he went he attracted favorable attention and publicity."[31] But it is characteristic that in the conclusions of a full length study of Athenagoras, no reference is made to any concern for social involvement of his church.[32] His strengths were great and formidable—but they did not include social concerns.

Archbishop Michael (Constantinides 1949-1958), a man of great spiritual stature was, not unexpectedly, also primarily and essentially concerned with the inner life of the Archdiocese. It can probably be said without fear of contradiction, that Archbishop Michael's strength was his concern for the spiritual growth of his church. His love for St. Paul was legendary. His translations of spiritual works such as Bound's, *The Power of Prayer,* and Fr. John of Kronstadt's, *My Life in Christ* (into Greek), are witnesses of this truth. Organizationally, he established the Greek Orthodox Youth of America, and one of his major concerns was to promote the use of the sacrament of Holy Confession among his people. The collected encyclicals of Archbishop Michael include fifty-three pages of encyclicals on 'Philanthropy' and fifty-five classified as "National and Social Issues."[33] The first of these consists mostly of encyclical appeals for funds for groups such as the American Red Cross, the Greek Red Cross, American Friends for the Blind in Greece, Save the Children Federation, Care, and appeals for financial aid to victims of disasters such as fires, earthquakes and hurricanes. Four topics referred to with some regularity are of special interest. One is the establishment, through the initiative of the First Archdiocesan District Clergy Association, of an old age home in New York. Another is a letter of support for a private group of Greek Orthodox women who were working for the establishment of an old age home in Massachusetts. A topic of repeated concern was the Watkins Immigration bill and the need for sponsors for 16,000 anticipated immigrants. The most interesting, however, for our study are the several encyclicals dealing with the establishment and functioning of a welfare department at the Archdiocese, announced in an encyclical of October 10, 1957,[34] which was to concern itself with all of the needs of our Greek Orthodox brethren which refer to hospitals, adoption, immigration questions of Greek-Americans" and "all kinds of socially beneficial purposes which are in harmony with the mission of the Church."

Of the encyclicals classified as dealing with "National and Social

Issues," about 83% of the total deal with clearly ethnic and national issues, such as the celebration of Greek Independence Day, the defiant 'Ochi' ('No') (to the Italian demand in 1940 for immediate capitulation of Greece to the Fascists) of October 28. A number of them, however, dealt with questions of Greek ethnic interests in regard to Cyprus, Northern Epiros, and the Anti-Greek riots in Istanbul in September 1965. The remaining seventeen percent dealt with a variety of topics such as the following: Greek War wounded aid, pastoral concern for Greek Orthodox Korean War draftees, Korean War blood drive; voter registration of Greek Orthodox American citizens; prayers for those behind the Iron Curtain; and the recognition of Greek Orthodoxy as a major faith in state legislatures.

Clearly, there was no concern for issues which dealt with topics common to the whole citizenry of the nation. Philanthropy and social concern were restricted to "our own" by and large, but ecclesial concern with the great social and moral issues affecting society as a whole was absent. There is clear evidence to verify that Christian Philanthropy and concern for human welfare is strongly present. But concern with general social issues would have to wait for its expression in the Greek Orthodox Archdiocese of North and South America.

However, Orthodox theology was beginning to respond to "the Social Question." Greek Orthodox theologians and other Orthodox theologians who have had some impact on Orthodox theological thought and education began to deal with these issues in one way or another primarily following the rise of communism in Russia and other Eastern European nations. Thus, some university theology professors, such as Fr. Vafeides, Demetrios Balanos, Hamilcar Alivizatos and Gregorios Papamichael and others, dealt with economic and social justice questions from an Orthodox Christian perspective in the 1920's and 1930's.[35] The first part of the 1940's was a very difficult period since Greece was occupied by the Axis powers. Starvation and suffering were rampant. Yet, in this period, or perhaps because of it, a quiet yet remarkable development took place. A group of Greek Orthodox theologians, scientists and scholars organized themselves in the summer of 1943 into a study group called "The Christian Social Circle." The group met for a long time with the permission of the German authorities as a "Bible Study" group in a house directly across the street from the *Feld Kommandatur* in Athens with the full knowledge that their discussions were, in fact, illegal, and if discovered, would have caused not only dispersal of the group but would have been the occasion for severe punishment of the group members by the occupation authorities. The purpose of the group was to gather together Christian believers who wished to use their faith as a guiding light "to study the social problems, in the face of the expected liberation, with the purpose of contributing to the future general rehabilitation of our country." The sessions consisted of several papers and then specific decisions in the form of resolutions based on the discussions which followed the readings of the papers. The group met regularly every other week without detection, continuing on after the war. In 1951 a portion of the papers was published in a book, edited by the University of Athens' Old Testament professor, Panagiotes Bratsiotes, under the title, *The Social Problem and Christianity: Introductions and Conclusions of the Christian Social Circle: First Series.*[36] The Table of Contents is of interest: "Christianity, the Economy and Society," "The Idea of Christian Socialism," "Catholic Social Teaching," "The Application of Catholic Social Teaching in Portugal," "Christianity and Work," "Christianity and Property," "The Social Teaching of the Fathers of the Church," "Eugenics and Ethics." Included as well, were the resolutions adopted on the topics "Christianity and Property," "Christianity and Labor," "Christianity and Politics," "The Greek Educational Problem," "Church and State from a Greek Perspective," as well as a "Message . . . to the Christian Social Circles of Great Britain and the United States of America" following the conclusion of the war.

Many of the members of this study group went on to assume high posts in the post-war Greek governmental, economic, educational and ecclesial structures.

Thus, following the war, there was a prepared climate for dealing with social and moral issues. Analyses of the situation from specifically Orthodox Christian perspectives were made. For example, Alexander Tsirindanes published a series of articles on the post-war situation in the periodical *Aktines.*[37] Soon many articles and books followed, some of which were also published in English.[38]

Yet, hardly any of this interest and concern touched the Greek Orthodox scene in the Western hemisphere. The new climate of interest in problems of social and moral concern in the homeland, expressed among theologians and intellectuals in Greece, did not cross the ocean to America.

The major concerns of both Greek Orthodox leadership and laity was directed inwardly, as we have seen. Its two foci were internal organization and religio-ethnic identity. There was philanthropic concern, most of which was directed to the Greek community here and abroad, and some of which was clearly a response initiated from outside the Church. There was no expressed concern for the issues of social justice and concern regarding the nation at large, no grappling with the public issues of the time, no broad based social conscience in the Greek Orthodox Church of the Americas.

Such was the situation at the threshold of the tenure in the Americas of Archbishop Iakovos (Coucouzis) which began in 1959. What follows in this book is, in large part, a chronicle of the change in the Greek Orhtodox Church in North and South America regarding its perspective on moral and social issues. As will be seen, the role of Archbishop Iakovos in this — as in so many others — was pivotal.

He was well qualified for the task. Born on July 29, 1911, on the Turkish island of Imbros, he knew at first hand the 500-year tradition of oppression, enforced silence and the bitterness of "second-class citizenship." Immersed in the patriarchal tradition through his studies at the Ecumenical Patriarchate's Theological School at Halki, he graduated in 1934, having studied the broad and wide-ranged ethics of Professor Vasileios Antoniades, who was mentioned above. In the same year he was ordained deacon. A few years later, in 1939, he came to the United States to serve as Archdeacon and on the faculty of Holy Cross Greek Orthodox School of Theology, then located in Pomfret, Connecticut (now, since 1946, located in Brookline, Massachusetts).This association and concern for theological education has continued to be a lifelong preoccupation. Ordained a priest the following year, he began a period in his life in which he developed a sensitivity to the problems of the American Greek Orthodox Church. Between 1940 and 1954, he was a pastor, serving twelve of those years as Dean of the Annunciation Cathedral of Boston. During this period, he earned a Master of Sacred Theology degree from Harvard Divinity School. That pastoral experience, so richly informed by his new educational experience, was then powerfully enriched, broadened and deepened, when, upon his election as titular bishop of Melita in December of 1954, he assumed duties as the representative of the Ecumenical Patriarchate to the World Council of Churches in Geneva, Switzerland. This four-year post enabled him to voice a concern for the relationship of Orthodoxy to other faiths and to the problems which the Church was called upon to face in the twentieth century. Elected Archbishop of the Greek Orthodox Archdiocese of North and South America on February 14, 1959, and enthroned on April 1, 1959, he began a multifaceted ministry of great breadth. During the early years of his tenure here, he also served as a co-president of the World Council of Churches (1959-1968), while at the same time he recommended the establishment and had, since 1960, served as chairman of the Standing Conference of Canonical Orthodox Bishops in America.

This broad background contributed to an important new emphasis in the life of the Greek Orthodox Church in the Americas. It is true that similar to his predecessors, Archbishop Iakovos continued to expend great energy on the organizational and spiritual life of his church. It is also true that he focused much attention on the improvement and enrichment of inter-Orthodox cooperation, especially in the United States. No less an interest and concern was his ecumenical activity. He is well known for these concerns.

It is not so well known that over the past two decades he has had an important role in reorienting the attention and thought of his church to its long-dormant tradition of social concern. As a pastor of souls, several influences formed in him the social consciousness he sought to communicate to his flock: the ancient traditions of his birthplace, the burden of the non-Christian yoke of centuries, the enlightened ethical teaching of his Halki training, the pastoral experience in the New World, and the non-Orthodox and Orthodox [39] theological concern with social issues.

The Archbishop, of course, was not alone in these interests, but it was he who gave such outreach and concern a firm Orthodox Christian grounding for the Greek people in North America. Political activism is not unknown to the Greek-American community. Fraternal organizations abound among the Greeks. There are many associations of persons from specific regions of Greece, such as the Pan-Arcadians, the Pan-Cretans, and the Epirotic Society. In addition, during the early period of immigrant adaptation to America, several national associations came into being, the most prominent of which was the American-Hellenic Educational and Progressive Association (AHEPA). This organization performed yeoman work in promoting Greek interests in the political sphere. Though not unrelated to the Church (its members were nearly all Greek-Americans of the Orthodox faith), it charted an independent course in many of its endeavors.

The event which served to mobilize Greek Orthodox involvement in public issues to a never-before realized intensity was the tragedy of the Cyprus invasion by Turkish forces in July of 1974.

AHEPA and other fraternal and ethnic regional forces reacted, but the Archdiocese also entered into the fray to mobilize political forces on behalf of justice for Cyprus. This effort resulted in what has since become known as the "Greek Lobby" in Congress. Several organizations were created to mobilize ethnic political concerns. One is the American Hellenic Institute Public Affairs Committee, a lobbying group registered with the U.S. Congress, which seeks, among other things, to "strengthen congressional support for Greece and Cyprus in the light of U.S. interests and to involve the American Hellenic Community in direct participation in public affairs."[40] This group, as the membership of the boards of directors and trustees indicates, does not seem to have any formal connection with the Greek Orthodox Archdiocese. Its interests are strongly political.

A broader, more culturally and religiously based organization is the United Hellenic American Congress. Its beginning was also the Cyprus tragedy. The flurry of activity among Greek Orthodox people in support of Cyprus by both groups and individuals made it evident that "a coordinated and unified effort was needed."

> Out of this need emerged UHAC, Illinois Council, on January 28, 1975, when representatives of two major groups in the Chicago area met and agreed to form the umbrella organization. The example of the Chicago action was the springboard for the formation of UHAC on the national level which occurred on June 6, 1975. At that time, leaders of the Greek community met at Hellenic College in Brookline, Mass., and established the National United Hellenic Congress.[41]

Both the location of its founding (Hellenic College is the location of Holy Cross Greek Orthodox School of Theology) and its activities indicate a close relationship to the Church. In addition to political activity on behalf of Cyprus and Greece, it supports and coordinates many cultural events, has underwritten publications of concern to Greek Orthodox peoples and interests (e.g., *Turkey Violates Human Rights of Orthodox Christians and the Ecumenical Patriarchate of Constantinople*), supervised parades and rallies, maintained relationships with local and national political leaders, reported to the 24th Clergy-Laity Congress of the Greek Orthodox Church on its activities and, in general, closely identified with the life of the Greek Orthodox Church. UHAC may well be on the road to becoming a social concern agency of the Church — or it may only be an agency for the mobilization of the Greek American fraternal

and local organizations. It will depend much on the direction provided by its leadership.

With this background, we then turn attention to a more careful
examination of the formation of the social consciousness among
the Greek Orthodox, a process which we trace through the encyclicals, the keynote addresses and the decisions of the Social and
Moral Issues Committees of the Clergy-Laity Congresses of the
Greek Orthodox Archdiocese of the Americas over the decades of
the sixties and seventies.

NOTES

1. From the Vespers of Meatfare Sunday. *Triodion Katanyktikon* (Athens,
1967), p. 28, The Doxastikon of the Lite.

2. See, for example, 1 Corinthians 16. 1-4.

3. A few representative studies follow (I have sought to include the works
of Orthodox authors in order to document a continuing concern with these
issues): Savvas Agourides, *He koinoktemosyne en te prote Ekklesia* (Thessalonike, 1963); Cecil John Cadoux, *The Early Church and the World: A
History of the Christian Attitude to Pagan Society and the State Down to the
Time of Constantinus* (Edinburgh, 1925), parts 1, 2, 3; Igino Giordane, *The
Social Message of Jesus* (Boston, 1977); *idem, The Social Message of the Apos-
tles* (Boston, 1978); Georgios S. Gratseas, *He peri ptocheias didaskalia tes
Hagias Graphes* (Athens, 1962); Vasileios X. Ioannides, *To Evangelion kai to
koinonikon provlema* (Athens, 1957); Panagiotes Mpratsiotes, *Ho Iesous
Christos eto socialistes?* (Athens, 1925); *idem, He koinonike semasia tes
Palaias Diathekes* (Athens, 1952); Demosthenes Savramis, *Peri ergasias
didaskalias tou Apostolou Pavlou* (Athens, 1962); Ernst Troeltsch, *The
Social Teachings of the Christian Churches* (New York, 1931), chapter
1, section 1,2.

4. Cadoux, *Early Church*, part 1.

5. *Ibid.*, 2, 3.

6. Karl Holl, "The Missionary Methods of the Ancient and Medieval Church,"
The Unitarian-Universalist Christian, 31, nos. 3-4 (1976), pp. 31-32.

7. See, for instance: Cadoux, *Early Church* parts 4-6; Robert M. Grant,
Early Christianity and Society (New York, 1977); Nektarios Hatzimichales,
Ai peri idioktesias apopseis en te Ekklesia kata tous treis protous aionas
(Thessalonike, 1972); R. A. Norris, Jr., *God and World in Early Christian*

Theology: A Study in Justin Martyr, Irenaeus, Tertullian and Origen (New York); Ernest Troeltsch, *Social Teachings*, chpater 1, sec. 3.

8. These are the chapter headings of Panagiotes Demetropoulos, *He pistis tes archaias Ekklesias os kanon tes zoes kai ho kosmos* (Athens, 1959), which covers the first six centuries of the Christian era. See also, Igino Giordani, *The Social Message of the Early Fathers* (Boston, 1977).

9. These are chapter headings in Demetrios J. Constantelos, *Byzantine Philanthropy and Social Welfare* (New Brunswick, 1968).

10. Ernest Barker, *Social and Political Thought in Byzantium* (Oxford, 1957), pp. 54-63.

11. Panagiotes Chrestou, *He koinoniologia tou Megalou Vasileiou* (Athens, 1951).

12. Chrysostomos Baur, *John Chrysostom and His Time* (Westminster, 1959), 1, p. 38.

13. Ibid., pp. 377-78. See Homily 21, v. 5 on First Corinthians.

14. See, for example, Panagiotes G. Stamos, *Ioannou tou Chrysostomou, koinonikai homiliai: he kale ton chrematon chresis; ho ploutos eis ten hyperesian tes agapes* (Athens, 1964); *idem, Ioannou tou Chrysostomou, koinonikai homiliai B': he kake ton chrematon chresis; ho ploutos eis ten hyperesian tou ego* (Athens, 1968); *idem, Ioannou tou Chrysostomou, homiliai peri anatrophes teknon* (Athens, 1962); *idem, Ioannou tou Chrysostomou, gamos kai syzygia* (Athens, 1963).

15. L. J. Charnay, *Saint Jean Chrysostome; Moraliste* (Lyon, 1969); I. K. Conevskii, *Social Ideas in the Church Fathers I: St. John Chrysostom* (Sophia, 1948); Methodios Fougias, *The Social Message of St. John Chrysostom* (Athens, 1968).

16. This passage is based primarily on the account in Steven Runciman, *The Great Church in Captivity: A Study of the Patriarchate of Constantinople from the Eve of the Turkish Conquest to the Greek War of Independence* (Cambridge, 1968), pp. 185, 205.

17. Ibid.

18. Ibid., p. 186.

19. Ibid., p. 204-05.

20. Ioannes E. Anastasiou, "The Neomartyrs of the Greek Orthodox Church," *Alumni Lectures: Number Three* (Brookline, 1973), pp. 89-100.

21. Karl Holl, *Unitarian*, p. 35.

22. I. Alexios, D. Kioulhatzes, N. Logiades, et. al., *Ti prosephere ho christianismos 3: koinonike merimna sten Tourkokratia* (Athens, 1980).

23. Nomikos M. Vaporis, *Father Kosmas: The Apostle of the Poor* (Brookline, 1977), p. 6.

24. *Ibid.*, p. 7.

25. My own father, Samuel S. Harakas, remembers as a young man the liberation of his home island of Samos from the Turks by the Greek forces, and the poverty which the subsequent economic disruption caused.

26. Vasileios Antoniades, *Encheiredion kata Christon ethikes, tomos B' perilamvanon to eidikon meros* (Constantinople, 1927).

27. Chrestos Androutsos, *Systema Ethikes* (Athens, 1925).

28. Charles C. Moskos, Jr. *Greek Americans: Struggle and Success* (Englewood Cliffs, 1980), chapter seven, "The Sociology of Greek Americans."

29. Demetrios J. Constantelos, ed., *Encyclicals and Documents of the Greek Orthodox Archdiocese of North and South America Relating to Its Thought and Activity the First Fifty Years 1922-1972* (Thessalonike, 1976).

30. Ibid., pp. 415-75.

31. Peter T. Kourides, *The Evolution of the Greek Orthodox Church in America and Its Present Problems* (New York, 1959).

32. George Papaioannou, *From Mars Hill to Manhattan: The Greek Orthodox in America Under Patriarch Athenagoras I* (Minneapolis, 1976), pp. 270-77.

33. Constantelos, *Encyclicals,* pp. 591-643 and pp. 660-714.

34. Ibid., pp. 627-28.

35. A selected bibliography these writings is: Hamilcar Alivizatos, *He koinonike apostole tes Ekklesias* (Athens, 1934); *idem,* "He agape kai ta erga aftes en te archaia Ekklesia" *Gregorios Palamas,* 11 (1927); G. Delenga, "Ho Charakter tis koinoktemosynes tis protes christianikes Ekklesias," *Pantainos,* 29 (1937); G. Zacharoules, "He idioktesia, to dikaioma tes idioktesias, kai ta ex aftou agatha," *Pantainos* 23 (1931); *idem,* "Ho ploutos kai ho Christianismos," *Pantainos,* 29 (1937); M. Karapipere, "He kommounistike politeia tes protes christianikes epoches," *Nea Sion,* 15 (1920); Demetrios Mpalanos, "He romaike politeia kai ho Christianismos mechri ton meson tou 3ou aionos," *Theologia,* 1 (1923), 2 (1924); Gregorios Papamichael, "Pote oi plousioi einai axiokatakritoi," *Pantainos,* 4 (1912).

36. *To koinonikon provlema kai ho Christianismos: eisegeseis kai porismata tou Christianikou Kyklou: seira prote* (Athens, 1951). To my knowledge, the balance of the studies have not been published.

37. Stanley S. Harakas, "Alexander N. Tsirindanes on the present Age," *The Greek Orthodox Theological Review,* 2 (1956), pp. 75-82.

38. Some of the literature of Orthodox writers from the mid-1940s to the early 1960s is the following: Savvas Agourides, *Ho koinonikos charakter tes Orthodoxias* (Thessalonike, 1962); Gregorios S. Gratseas, *He peri ptocheias Didaskalia tes Hagias Graphes* (Athens, 1962); Panagiotes Demetropoulos, *He pistis tes archaias Ekklesias os kanon tes zoes kai ho kosmos* (Athens, 1959); Vasileios X. Ioannides, *To Evangelion kai to koinonikon provlema* 2nd ed.

(Athens, 1957); Spyridon M. Kalliapha, *Charakterismos tes epoches mas* (Athens, 1953); Demetrios I. Magriotes, *Synchrona provlemata tou Christianou* (Athens, 1964); P. Melites (Alexandros Tsirintanes), *Gia n' anoixe ho dromos* (Athens, 1957); Panagiotes Mpratsiotes, "He koinonike didaskalia tou Apostolou Pavlou," *Aktines*, 14 (1951); *idem, He koinonike semasia tes Palaias Diathekes* (Athens, 1952); Anastasios Pieros, *Ho koinonismos tou Christianismou* (Athens, 1963); Polykarpos of Messenia, "He koinoktemosyne kai he christianike threskeia," *Ekklesia* (1953); D. Stephanides, "Christianismos kai idioktesia," *Praktika tou Syndreiou Hellenochristianikou Politismou* (Athens, 1956); Demetrios Tsakonas, *Koinonia kai Orthodoxia* (Athens, 1956); (Alexander Tsirintanes), *Towards A Christian Civilization: A Draft Issued by the Christian Union of Professional Men of Greece* (Athens, 1950); Andreas I. Phytrakes, *Oi Monachoi os koinonikoi didaskaloi dai ergatai en te archaia anatolike Ekklesia* (Athens, 1950); Panagiotes Chrestou, *He koinoniologia tou Megalou Vasileiou* (Athens, 1951).

39. A selection of some recent writings in this area by Orthodox authors will serve to illustrate the point: Savas Agourides, "The Social Character of Orthodoxy," *The Greek Orthodox Review*, (1962-63), pp. 7-20. Reprinted in A. J. Philippou, ed. *The Orthodox Ethos* (Oxford, 1964), pp. 209-20; Paul B. Anderson, "Religious Liberty Under Communism," *A Journal of Church and State*, 6 (1964), pp. 169-77; Michael Azkoul, "Prolegomena to a Critique of Western Culture," *Greek Orthodox Theological Review*, 4 (1958-1959), pp. 151-60; *idem*, "The Greek Fathers: Polis and Paideia," *St. Vladimir's Theological Quarterly*, 23 (1979), pp. 3-21, 67-86; Evgeny Barabanov, "The Ethical Prerequisite for Christian Unity," *St. Vladimir's Theological Quarterly*, 18 (1974), pp. 128-37; Nicholas Berdyaev, "Ho threskevtikos Messianismos tou rossikou Kommounismou," *Synoron*, No. 40, 1966-1970, pp. 268-73; Elizabeth Behr-Sigel, "The Participation of Women in the Life of the Church," *Sobornost*, series 7: no. 6 (1978), pp. 480-92; Demetrios J. Constantelos, *Byzantine Philanthropy and Social Welfare* (New Brunswick) 1968; *idem, Marriage, Sexuality and Celibacy, A Greek Orthodox Perspective* (Minneapolis, 1975); *idem*, "A Note on 'Christos Philanthropos' in Byzantine Iconography," *The Greek Orthodox Theological Review*, 21 (1976), pp. 158-62; *idem*, "Physician-Priests in the Medieval Greek Church," *The Greek Orthodox Theological Review*, 12 (1966-67), pp. 141-53; *idem*, "The Social Ethos of the Orthodox Church," in *God and Charity: Images of Eastern Orthodox Theology, Spirituality, and Practice*, ed. Francis D. Costa. (Brookline, 1979), pp. 75-87; *idem*, "Social Consciousness in the Greek Orthodox Church," *The Greek Orthodox Theological Review*, 12 (1967), pp. 306-39; *idem*, "Theological Considerations for the Social Ethos of the Orthodox Church," in *Meletemata ste mneme Vasileiou Laourda* (THessalonike, 1975), pp. 323-35; *Christian Obedience and the Search for Liberation: An Orthodox Perspective*. Papers of the 2nd International Consultation of Orthodox Youth and Students, Cairo, September 22-27, 1978 (Geneva, 1979); Athanasios Delikostopoulos, *He Ekklesia enanti ton ragdaion koinonikon kai technikon*

exelixeon tou synchronou kosmou (Athens, 1969); Paul Evdokimov, "The Social Dimension of Orthodox Ecclesiology," *Theology Digest*, 18 (1970), pp. 43-52; George Fedotov, "The Church and Social Justice," *St. Vladimir's Seminary Quarterly*, 7 (1963); Georges Florovsky, *Christianity and Culture*, Vol. 2, in the *Collected Works* (Belmont, Mass., 1974). In particular the Chapters on "Faith and Culture," "Antimonies of Christian History: Empire and Desert," "Christianity and Civilization," and "The Social Problem in the Eastern Orthodox Church."; Geroglios S. Gratseas, *He peri ptocheias didaskalia tes Hagias Graphes* (Athens, 1962); Paulos Gregorios, *The Human Presence: An Orthodox View of Nature* (Geneva, 1978); Stanley S. Harakas, (nom de plume: "Exetastes"), *Contemporary Issues: Orthodox Christian Perspectives* (New York, 1976); *idem, For the Health of Body and Soul: An Eastern Orthodox Introducation to Bioethics* (Brookline, 1980); *idem,* "Alexander N. Tsirindanes on the Present Age," *The Greek Orthodox Theological Review*, 7 (1961-1962), pp. 92-105; *idem,* "The Orthodox Theological Approach to Modern Trends," *St. Vladimir's Theological Quarterly*, 13 (1969), pp. 198-211; *idem,* "He Ethike Didaskalia tou Pentekostariou" (The Ethical Teaching of the Pentecostarion) *Theologia*, 39 (1968), pp. 368-85 and pp. 586-612; *idem,* "An Orthodox Approach to the New Morality," *The Greek Orthodox Theological Review*, 27 (1980), pp. 107-39; *idem,* "The Church and the Secular World," *Greek Orthodox Theological Review*, 17 (1972); *idem,* "Greek Orthodox Ethics and Western Ethics," *Journal of Ecumenical Studies*, 10 (1973), pp. 728-51; *idem,* "Ennoia tis prosarmoges tes Orthodoxias eis ton synchronon kosmon," *Epistemonike Epiteris Theologikes Scholes Panepistemiou Thessalonikes: Diorthodoxou Theologikon Symposion 12-16 Septerbriou, 1972 Special Issue*, 19 (1974), pp. 125-40; *idem,* "Orthodox Church-State Theory and American Democracy," *Greek Orthodox Theological Review*, 21 (1976), pp. 399-401; *idem,* "Population: An Eastern Orthodox Perspective," *Encyclopedia of Bioethics*, New York, 1978, Vol. 3, pp. 1251-54; *idem,* "Eastern Orthodox Medical Ethics," *Encyclopedia of Bioethics*, (New York, 1978), vol. 1, pp. 341-46; *idem,* "Reflections on the Ethical Demensions of the Topics of the Great and Holy Synod," *Greek Orthodox Theological Review*, 24 (1979), pp. 131-57; Haralambos Hatzopoulos, *To provlema tis autocheirias* (Athens, 1969); Vasil T. Istavridis, "The Concept of the Nature of Men and Women Which Allows Us to Envisage Partnership," *Greek Orthodox Theological Review*, 7 (1961-1962), pp. 14-21; Ioannis O. Kalogerou, "Ho Megas Basileios hypodeigma christianou koinonikou ergatou," in *Basileias: Heoratios Tomos Epi te Symplerosei 1600 Eton apo tou Thanatou tou M. Basileiou* (Thessalonike, 1979); Georgiou A. Kapsane, *He poimantike merimna tis Ekklesias hyper tou phylakismenon* (Athens, 1969); Issa J. Khalil, "The Ecological Crisis: An Eastern Christian Perspective," *St. Vladimir's Theological Quarterly*, 22 (1978), pp. 193-211; Georges Khodr, "Christianity in a Pluralistic World," *Sobornost*, Series 6, No. 3, 1971, pp. 166-74; *idem,* "The Church and the World," *St. Vladimir's Theological Quarterly*, 18 (1969), pp. 33-51; Jerome Kotsonis, "Fundamental

Principles of Orthodox Morality," *The Orthodox Ethos*, ed. by A. J. Philippou (Oxford, 1964), pp. 229-48; Chrysostomos Konstantinides, "Technike goni-mopoiesis kai theologia," *Orthodoxia*, 33 (1955); 34 (1956); John Kowalzyk, *An Orthodox View of Abortion* (Minneapolis, 1977); George I. Mantzarides, *He christianike koinonia kai ho kosmos* (Thessalonike, 1967); *idem, Christianike koinoniologia* (Thessalonike, 1973); *idem, Themata koinoniologias tis Orthodoxias* (Thessalonike, 1975); *idem, Koinoniologia tou Christianismou* (Thessalonike, 1981); *idem,* "To ethikon noema tou peri Triados dogmatos," *Kleronomia*, 1 (1969), pp. 233-46; *idem,* "The Witness of Orthodoxy to the Contemporary World," *St. Vladimir's Theological Quarterly*, 17 (1973), pp. 170-80; Nicholas E. Metsopoulos, *Physis kai latrevtikos charakter ton agathon ergon* (Athens, 1969); John Meyendorff, *Marriage: An Orthodox Perspective* (Crestwood, N. Y., 1970); Konstantin Muchulsky, "The Idea of Social Christianity in Russian Philosophy" *St. Vladimir's Seminary Quarterly*, 12 (1968), pp. 157-69; Panagiotes Nellas, "Treis biblikes prohypo-theseis yia ten prosengisi tou thematos tis politkes," *Synoro*, No. 40 (1966-1967), pp. 186-302; Nicos A. Nissiotis, "Church and Society in Greek Orthodox Theology," in *Christian Social Ethics In A Changing World*, ed. John C. Bennett (New York, 1966); Elias Oikonomou, *Theologike theoresis ton problematon tou perivallontos* (Athens, 1973); *The Orthodox Approach to Diaconia: Consultation of Church and Service,* (Geneva, 1980); Stylianos Papadopoulos, *Hagiotis kai koinonikotes* (Athens, 1968); George D. Rodites, *Christianimos kai ploutos* (Athens, 1970); John S. Romanides, "Remarks of an Orthodox Christian on Religious Freedom," *Greek Orthodox Theological Review,* 8 (1962-63), pp. 127-32; *idem,* "The Orthodox Churches on Church State Relations and Religious Liberty," *A Journal of Church and State*, 6 (1964), pp. 178-89; Demosthenes Savrames, *He peri ergasias didaskalia tou Apostolou Pavlou* (Athens, 1962); Phillip Sherrard, "Humanae Vitae: An Orthodox Comment," *Sobornost*, Series 5, no. 8 (1969), pp. 570-80; Vladimir Solovyov, "He orthodoxe christologia gia ta koinonika provlemata," *Synoro,* no. 40 (1966-67), pp. 280-86; Dumitru Staniloae, "Christian Responsibility in the World," *The Tradition of Life, Studies Supplementary to Sobornost,* no. 2, ed. A. M. Allchin (London, 1971); Alexander M. Stavropoulos, *To provlema tes teknogonias ke he engyklios tes ekklesias tis Hellados (1937)* (Athens, 1977); Euthymios K. Stylios, *To synchronon astikon perivallon os poimantikon provlema* (Athens, 1980); Emilianos Timiadis, "Restoration and Liberation in and by the Community," *The Greek Orthodox Theological Review,* 19 (1974), pp. 131-58; Alexander N. Tsirintanes, *Knowing Where We Are Going: Contemporary Problems and the Christian Faith*, tr. George A. Perris (London, 1977); Kallistos Ware, "The Value of Material Creation," *Sobornost,* series 6, No. 3(1971), pp. 154-65; Chrestos Yannaras, "Orthodoxy and the West," *The Greek Orthodox Theological Review,* 17 (1972), pp. 115-31; Nicholas Stephen Webster, "Marxism and the Modern Revolution from an Orthodox Christian Perspective," *St. Vladimir's Theological Quarterly*, 24 (1980); *idem,* "The Canonical Validity of Military Service by Orthodox

Christians," *The Greek Orthodox Theological Review*, 23 (1978), pp. 257-81; Nikolai A. Zabolotsky, "Diakonia and Social Responsibility of the Church," *The Journal of the Moscow Patriarchate*, no. 9 (1980), pp. 68-77; Chrysostom Zaphiris, "The Morality of Contraception: An Eastern Orthodox Opinion," *Journal of Ecumenical Studies*, XI (1974), pp. 677-90.

40. From the AHI-PAC brochure.

41. *United Hellenic American Congress Update: A Brief Listing of the Activities of UHAC from 1975 to the Present (1980)*, p. 1.

Chapter Two

SOCIAL CONCERN IN THE ENCYCLICALS
OF ARCHBISHOP IAKOVOS

On Monday, March 15, 1965, in the Alabama city of Selma, a great crowd of people filled Brown Chapel for a memorial service for the Rev. James Reeb, a Unitarian minister from Boston, who had died as a result of a racist-inspired beating in Selma. It was to be held there because no permission had been received to conduct the service at the courthouse, where they had hoped to make it a public occasion to further the civil rights struggle of the nation's Blacks. The participants were waiting for Dr. Martin Luther King to speak to them. They waited for three hours before he arrived, accompanied by some distinguished personages, including the Greek Orthodox archbishop of North and South America. Archbishop Iakovos joined hands on the platform with the other spiritual leaders and sang some civil rights songs. He also spoke briefly in memory of the fallen civil rights leader. A few minutes later, the Rev. Ralph Abernathy announced in dramatic fashion that Federal Judge Daniel Thomas had just ordered the city to permit the gathered people to march in procession to the steps of the court-house and conduct the memorial service there. The service was to be brief—it did not, in fact, last a full twenty minutes—and was to consist only of a prayer, a brief homily by Dr. King, and a single chorus of "We Shall Overcome."

It was an emotional moment. Formal agreement was reached that the huge throng was to march three abreast. The line marched down Sylvan Street and turned the corner onto Alabama Avenue, through the main part of the city, to the Dallas County Court-house steps. They were met with the locking of the doors from within and by the extinguishing of the courthouse's outside lights. As the people positioned themselves, "Dr. King walked up the steps accompanied by Walter Reuther, Archbishop Iakovos of the Greek Orthodox Church and several other notables."[1] Much came out of that march, which was to lead to momentous decisions in the White House, the Supreme Court of the United States, and the Congress. One of the most memorable items, however, for the Orthodox Christians of this nation was the *Life* magazine cover of March 26, 1965, which depicted, side by side, the labor leader, the Black minister, and the traditionally robed Greek Orthodox archbishop, providing an image of unity which spoke eloquently for the concept of equal rights for all. And for the Orthodox of this nation, that photograph identified Archbishop Iakovos as a churchman, an Orthodox hierarch, and a spiritual leader with a social conscience and mission.

This chapter, in brief fashion, seeks to document that fact by focusing on one of many possible sources, the encyclicals of Archbishop Iakovos issued during the period 1959-1979. Besides this limitation, I have also deliberately excluded from this study clearly ethnically oriented issues, actions, and programs designed to promote patriotic feelings. However, there is a goodly amount of genuine social concern and action reflected in some ethnically related issues. I have used as the criterion for the inclusion of some ethnically related material an assessment of the motivation for the issuance of the encyclicals. Much response to and action on ethnic questions can be elicited on the basis of motives of ethnic pride rather than on the primary motive of Christian philanthropy and social concern. Without a doubt, this is slippery ground. It would not be honest to divorce the ethnic from the ethical, or national and cultural sentiments from Christian values of love and philanthropy. In Greek Orthodox history, they simply cannot be separated. Yet, for obvious reasons, it would be equally unfair to characterize every expression of concern with nationally and culturally related issues as based on purely Christian motives, so I have chosen not to include ethnic expressions of clear patriotic motivation in order to isolate those aspects concerned with philanthropy and social justice.

The Socially Concerned Encyclicals

The role of the bishop in the Church is central to its existence. Though the threefold work of Christ as prophet, king, and high priest is exercised by the whole Church, in Orthodox ecclesiology all these tasks are under the mantle of the bishop. The priests (presbyters) derive their authority and *raison d'être* from the bishop, and the laity ultimately find direction from him.[2]

The prophetic, or teaching, role of the bishop need not be

documented or justified theologically at this point, since it is self-evident. The great bishops among the Fathers of the Church are particularly notable for their teaching. In general, the chief vehicles for the exercise of the teaching ministry have been the sermon and the encyclical.

Over the first twenty-year period of Archbishop Iakovos' leadership of the Greek Orthodox Archdiocese of North and South America, there was a prodigious production of encyclicals issued for the direction, correction, guidance, and inspiration of the faithful. The chief source of the encyclicals of the primates of the Greek Orthodox Archdiocese of North and South America is the monumental work, edited by Demetrios J. Constantelos, *Encyclicals and Documents of the Greek Orthodox Archdiocese of North and South America Relating to Its Thought and Activity, The First Fifty Years (1922-1972).*[3] Quantitatively, the encyclicals listed in this work for each of the primates is impressive. Constantelos devotes 79 pages to the eight years of Archbishop Alexander's primacy; 369 pages to the seventeen-year primacy of Archbishop (later Ecumenical Patriarch) Athenagoras; 223 pages to the nine years of service of Archbishop Michael; and 537 pages of encyclicals to the first thirteen years of Archbishop Iakovos' tenure as archbishop of North and South America. These encyclicals were written for many occasions on various topics and have been organized by Constantelos under the following subject headings: administration, interchurch relations, pastoral matters, philanthropy, youth, education, national and social issues.[4]

In addition to this major resource, the archives of the archdiocese have preserved a substantial number of encyclicals pertinent to our subject, inclusive of the encyclicals from 1973 to 1978, thus providing source material for the twenty-year primacy of Archbishop Iakovos.[5]

These encyclicals represent a significant aspect of the teaching ministry of the Church during the twenty-year period under discussion. It is not the purpose of this study to analyze or evaluate the evidence of social concern shown in these encyclicals. Rather, we limit ourselves simply to reporting on the existence of social concern in the encyclicals of Archbishop Iakovos, leaving for a later date and, perhaps, to others, a systematic analysis of their content and development. Our purpose here is only to document their existence, to identify and locate them for the purpose of investigating the dimensions of social concern in the encyclicals of Archbishop Iakovos during the period specified.

Assessments of the Social Condition

Running through the encyclicals of this period are short[6] evaluations of our present social climate. There is, of course, a perennial tendency on the part of preachers and teachers of the Christian Church to view the contemporary spiritual situation pessimistically. Yet, in Greek Orthodox social ethics thought, there has been a trend which has branded our age as an "Epoch of Negation," according to which the "spiritual negation" of the era after World War I in literature, arts, philosophy, morality, and religion has caused serious problems in the social sphere.[7] The encyclicals of Archbishop Iakovos express this same kind of assessment. Behind them is the conviction that moral and spiritual negation—in the form of the denial of its own Christian foundations by Western civilization—is the chief cause of the evils of our age.

The following passage from the Christmas encyclical of 1976 is a sample of the archbishop's analysis of the moral climate of our times. It brings to the attention of the flock a wide range of social problems.

To trust all our hopes to time or fate or secular leaders—a habit that is as old as man himself—does little credit to the enlightened contemporary Christian. It ranks him along with men of more benighted times and marks him as a fatalist. And a fatalist is slothful and unwilling when challenged to make some personal contribution to the betterment of the human condition. It is an attitude that fails against the immense problems of our time: abolishing social injustice; eliminating hunger; establishing the foundations of world peace; putting an end to violence and terrorism in the relations of people and nations.

All ideologies have been tried and found wanting as every political, social economic and even educational system. Tradition has been written off. The usefulness of history as mankind's tutor has been demeaned. All the antichrists have in their turn been hailed as the Christ. Agnosticism, secularism, even satanism—all have been installed on the altar of worship. Our age is awash in that indolent fatalism of all "mystic" religions, which defaulted and died where they sprang up. Cynicism and hedonism have been elevated to the dignity of ethical and philosophical systems. Euthanasia and abortion, along with homosecuality and moral perversion, have become a preoccupation even of religious denominations in this country. It is no wonder we are harvesting the bitter fruits of moral alienation: crime, violence, suicide—in short, death in all its grisly guides.[8]

For further expressions of this critical assessment of our times see: Prayer for President Johnson, Nov. 27, 1963; Feast of the Nativity, 1973; Thanksgiving, 1973, Nov. 9, 1973; Christmas, 1975; New Ecclesiastical Year 1976, Sept. 14, 1976; Christmas, 1978.[9]

General Social Concern

However, the encyclicals of this period do not merely indulge in hand-wringing. Again and again, the attention of the flock is directed to the issues of social concern. Belying the general impression that Eastern Orthodoxy is a faith which is turned inward, exclusively preoccupied with prayer and worship, the encyclicals of Archbishop Iakovos repeatedly focus on the great themes of social concern. Here, for example, is how the archbishop directs the attention of his flock in a Thanksgiving encyclical for 1968.

Thanksgiving Day is essentially a day of recollection, a time for reflecting in deep humility on our responsibilities, both as individuals and children of God, and as citizens of the richest and most powerful nation on earth.

As you well know, vast poverty and great injustice persist in the world. The weak are still exploited: wealth and power are still abused. There is still great waste of the earth's goods and neglect of spiritual and moral good. The substance of all these wrongs is a condemnation against us, since God fashioned the world as a place of joy in which man could perfect himself, not a place of torment where man would be debased.

As Christians we must be capable of examining ourselves, of reappraising the "given good things"; but also the freedom given us to acquire the "good things not given: trust and love and regard for those who are unjustly dealt with.

"For the Kingdom of God is not meat and drink, but righteousness and peace and joy in the Holy Spirit" (Rom. 14.17). Let us, therefore, ask ourselves on this Thanksgving Day what what we have done to insure justice, peace, and love in the world. Our conscience raises the question. And the more promptly we make a response, the better it will be for us, the better it will be for our world. [10]

In another encyclical, directed to the youth of the Church, after extensive discussion of the issue of the pollution of the environment, he draws his readers' attention to a litany of social concerns:

This, my beloved children in Christ, is my message to you on this Youth Sunday. In the unending stream of historical events, let us resolve to dedicate ourselves to the end of pollution and hence to be co-workers with God and perpetuators rather than defilers of His creative law. Let us also resolve to do the same with our own personal lives in the context of current historical events, that is to say, let us engage ourselves in the fight against other types of pollution, a pollution which is moral and social in nature, a pollution which is characterized by a negation of Orthodox Christian values and principles, and a pollution which is circumstanced by phenomena such as war, hate, prejudice, racism, sexual immorality, drug and alcoholic abuse, and an apathy and evolution amongst Orthodox Christian people toward their Church. Let us resolve this Youth Sunday to renew and live our Orthodox Faith. [11]

Appeals to Social Action

The kerygmatic character of many of the encyclicals, as we have seen, lends itself easily to pastoral exhortation. It is important to note that the encyclicals consistently concern themselves with the need for action, to the raising of the consciences of the faithful to deeds as well as words. Of course, these are words as well. Yet they provide a base for social action by extending the concern of the Church beyond the mere repetition of formulas. Thus, in the Easter encyclical for 1977, the archbishop calls for the development of "reasoned and moral solutions" to the world's problems as well as action leading to the "feeding of the hungry and defending the wronged." [12] In a wide ranging Thanksgiving encyclical for 1978 that strong sense of need, not only for words but for action as well, is expressed in the appeal that we "act out our Christian responsibility."

In this wondrous age that possesses all things, there are people who literally starve. In this age when we have learned to make the desert bloom, to turn the brackish seas into sweet water, there are those who thirst. In an age when so much is spoken of love and justice, dignity and peace, there are those who have not the remotest awareness of these things. Yet we enjoy all these benefits. We lack but one thing: the realization that we can and must share them with those who are deprived of them. However much "good" we do, it is the very least of what we should be doing.

Therefore, on this day of Thanksgiving, let us open up the circle of our table and broaden the compass of our thinking and caring. Let us set aside a portion for all who want for food, for hope, for help. Whether they be near or far, if there is room in our hearts for brotherly love, it will bring them all within that compass; those who are in America, as well as those who live in Asia or Africa or in the world's farthest reaches. Let us dedicate a portion for the Indians—a portion of love and gratitude. Let us save out a portion of compassion for our black and Hispanic brothers in areas of urban decay. Let us consecrate a portion of sympathy for the forgotten of war. Let us save a portion of succor for the victims of earthquake and flood and the orphans begotten of conflict. And let us find a place deep in our hearts for the Mideast, for Cyprus, for Rhodesia and Cambodia, where the struggle is for survival and justice.

Only as we perceive and feel and act out our Christian responsibility can Thanksgiving Day be a day of joy and gladness. Such is the Thanksgiving Day I wish you, one of joy and gladness, graced with "every perfect gift" from a loving Father.[13]

Human Rights

Many of the encyclicals, especially those having to do with the violation of political rights, contain frequent appeals to the rights people enjoy as human beings by virtue of their creaturehood as children of God. This concern for human rights reached white-hot intensity with the involvement of the archdiocese and Greek-Americans in general in the Cypriot issue, especially following the Turkish invasion and occupation of Cyprus in 1974. The festering issue of Cyprus, however, had long before that attracted the attention of Archbishop Iakovos. In an advent Christmas Lent encyclical dated Nov. 10, 1964, attention was focused on Cyprus and the resultant pressures of the Turkish authorities on the Greek population of Istanbul. This was followed two days later by a related news release on the expulsion of the Orthodox Christians from Turkey and extensive quoting from a *New York Times* editorial of November 11 entitled: "Innocent Victims," in which the deportations were characterized as "violations of human rights." It is significant that the news release takes credit for bringing this issue to the attention of the media. The Greeks in Cyprus are characterized by the encyclical as "those who are engaged in the sacred struggle for their self-determination."[14] A similar concern for the human rights of the Greek minority in Turkey led to an appeal to the United Nations Charter and to President Johnson's moral sensibilities. It was expressed in a communiqué entitled, "Vehement Protest of His Eminence Archbishop Iakovos Against the Persecution of the Greeks of Turkey and the Measures Against the Revered Ecumenical Patriarchate."[15]

The concern for human rights in a specific context, however, is not limited to Turkey and Cyprus. In July of 1978, Archbishop Iakovos sent a "telegram of outrage" to President Carter and Chairman Brezhnev concerning the "denial of basic human rights" to Anatoly Scharansky, Alexander Ginsburg, and Victoras Pyatkus, which included an appeal to the Helsinki Declaration.[16]

More generally, human rights is a frequent theme of Archbishop Iakovos in other contexts. An interesting example is to be found in a passage on "Human Dignity" in the March 25 celebration encyclical for 1971. I place this quotation here not because there are no others which speak more directly to human rights, but in order to illustrate the respect for humanity which must precede all appeals to human rights to avoid sloganeering.

By the term "dignity of man," no outward and frivolous niceties are implied. Man's need for dignity springs from the very essence of his being.

Dignity is the essence of life itself and from it alone is derived the right of man to call himself son of God. Not one of the institutions of man can stand alone without it: whether it be the family, society, the Church, education, or civilization itself. Institutions are to serve people but if they do not help the individual to be free, and to remain free and self-respecting to feel that he is truly the son of God, the brother of and equal to all others, they do not serve their own purpose. Exploitation, discrimination, social injustice—all are those indomitable forces, characteristic of, but which inevitably bring about the downfall of the reign of the rulers of the darkness of this age.[17]

Freedom

One of the most frequent themes in the encyclicals of this period is freedom. Several annual topics readily lend themselves to the treatment of this topic. Most common are the encyclicals on the

25th of March celebration, which highlights the Feast of the Annunciation and the celebration of Greece's Independence Day, and the encyclicals of Ochi Day, October 28, celebrating the famous "No" of Greece to Mussolini's 1940 demand that the nation surrender to a Fascist takeover. The former holiday lends itself traditionally to a twofold interpretation of freedom, spiritual and political.

However, as one reviews the encyclicals, it is clear that the concept of freedom is not limited to these celebrations, but occurs in many other contexts as well. However, in the March 25 and October 28 encyclicals the concept of freedom dominates, and it appears that a concerted effort has been made over the years to present as many varied aspects of it as possible. It would be a worthwhile effort to study these encyclicals in order to present a systematic treatment of the concept of freedom contained in them, a project which lies outside the scope of this study. Some of the views expressed are on the theoretical side, some more on the political side, but all are communicated passionately and forcefully. Thus, this powerful passage: "Freedom is not a deception but rather an exaltation. It is not an accident of history, but rather the natural state of God's children."[18]

An example of the weaving of various themes into the development of the theme of freedom is to be found in the March 25 celebration encyclical for 1976. I quote it rather extensively to give the reader a feeling for the power and strength of conviction expressed.

> ". . .And you will know the truth,
> and the truth will make you free."
> (John 8.32)

Truth and freedom unknown to those who live in falsehood and under its thrall, are as intimately bound together as love and justice. These four forces, and forces they are, are powerful and invincible and show us the meaning and the reality of life and polity in Christ.

The Christian life and polity alone lead to true freedom: that spiritual and moral freedom, in the absence of which political and national liberty have neither substance nor continuity. America won her struggle for independence with the watchword, "In God we trust." Declaring "we struggle for Christ's holy faith and the fatherland's freedom," the Greek nation, enslaved for 400 years, proved victorious in its titanic struggle against the presumably all-powerful and far-flung Ottoman Empire.

If today we have come to define and claim liberty, or rather liberties, not in the name of humanity, and certainly not in God's name, but only in the name of self, we had best take care lest we prove ultimately unworthy even of those "inalienable rights" and thus lose our very political freedom. And I fear such a danger exists; that under the tattered mantle of our abrogated religious faith as the force that orders men's lives, there lurks the specter of anarchy and communism, a system destructive of all meaning of human liberty.

Let us not forget that we were "bought with a price" (1 Cor. 7.23), that veritable rivers of blood were spilled for American and Greek independence. And if it is true that blood is the costliest and most priceless thing in the world, it is also true that none is more severely punished than he who deems the blood of Christ to be "common and of no value," and by the same token disdains the blood of those who have fought for freedom. "Do you not suppose that a much worse punishment is due the man who disdains the Son of God, thinks the covenant-blood by which he was sanctified to be ordinary, and insults the Spirit of grace" (Heb. 10.29). It follows that we ought to respect the blood by which freedom was bought and guard zealously that freedom "[for which] Christ has set us free" (Gal.5.1).

Today freedom, human freedom, that divine gift that nourishes and sustains human dignity, "God's image in us," is being eroded from within. What is more tragic is that it is being undermined by those very people who clamor for freedom. Men and women, in disturbingly large numbers, label freedom the repudiation of the established order: that moral, spiritual, social and political order that the centuries have tested. And yet, though they stray ever further from it, they seem incapable of achieving freedom and equality through license, which is their distorted conception of liberty. On the contrary, they destroy without creating, tear down without ever building up. Because they pursue equality only through means that annul and obliterate man's moral and spiritual personality, not in ways that ennoble and uplift the manner of life and stamp it as Christian.

We cannot march with the sloganeers. As people of 1976, it is fitting that we follow only the true freedom-fighters. We hark not to the false war cries of terrorists, but to the watch-words that express reverence for freedom, that safeguard our Greek, our American, and our Christian heritage. Let no one infer from the tepid spiritual and patriotic climate of the times that we are craven or disorganized, or lack the will to preserve what we regard as God's blessing and gift. On this day, the Day of the Annunciation, echoing the Church's command: "pro-claim day by day our God's salvation," let us proclaim with all our strength that we believe in one thing alone—truth, which is God; and freedom, which is the supreme expression of His Love for man.[19]

Finally, only passing reference can be made to an encyclical which focuses directly on the consequences of the political denial of freedom. In the March 25, 1978 encyclical, passionate refer-ence is made to "the subjugation and oppression of man" in the "slogans and banners of so-called socialist republics" that "crush people into nameless masses," exercising "mind control" and de-fining peace as the people's "submission to their will."[20]

Hunger

A recurring theme in the encyclicals is concern for the hungry throughout the world. In 1975, Archbishop Iakovos established a "World Hunger Fund" for the Archdiocese. Reference to the need for a Christian response to the problem of world hunger is found in encyclicals whose occasions are diverse: Great Lent, Easter, and Thanksgiving. An encyclical of remarkable breadth was issued for the 1975 Easter observance, with a focus on world hunger, and the fitting response of well-fed Christians to this fearsome reality. In the poetic style characteristic of most of his Easter messages, Archbishop Iakovos writes:

As we set out, under the wondrous radiance of the Unwaning light, which turns our steps toward the life in Christ where concern for equality and justice for man, God's image, ranks above all else, let us turn our enlightened and compassionate gaze on our hungry brothers: those who live among us, victims in a sense of our own insensitivity; those who live in far places —in Cyprus, Asia, Africa, Indochina, India—in every corner of the earth, who long to see in our Christianity the tenderness of Christ, in our advanced civilization the marks of a highly developed ethic, not merely a superior technology.

And when in a little while we stand before our heavily laden Easter table and make the sign of the Cross and sing the 'CHRISTOS ANESTI' (Christ is Risen), before we reach for the food, let us listen again to the St. John Chrysostom Easter homily, reminding us that: "The fatted calf is ample; no man should go away hungry." Only then should our hand reach forth —but controlled by our heart—and set aside the first portion for the destitute and starving of the world, thus giving substance to the Lord's desire, that "no man should go away hungry."

Then, eyes filled with stars, faces glistening like the dewy morning star, let us ask as many as we are able into our home, the dwelling place of Christ, and to our table, Christ's table, inviting all with brotherly love to: "partake of the feast of faith ...enjoy the riches of goodness..." And then let us light our paschal candle and illuminate the countenances of the poor with this assurance: "No man need lament his poverty for the universal kingdom has been proclaimed;" and joining hands let us sing "Christ is risen from the dead" in such a manner that "heaven and earth" shall be filled with the life-giving glow of the Resurrection.[21]

Family

A significant number of encyclicals express concern for the family, its stability in our times, and the consequences of its breakdown. An example of such concern is provided by the encyclical issued on the occasion of National Family Week, May 7-14, 1972. The suggestions for the observance of the week referred to below include suggested sermon topics, Sunday School essays, midweek dialogue-discussions, Family Holy Communion Sunday, bulletin announcements, Family Night Program, family discussions, etc.

Home and family life is the bedrock of our Greek Orthodox life-style. The spirit that binds us together as a people finds its deepest roots in the home where the tenderest values of human existence, love, compassion, forbearance and mutual helpfulness thrive in abundance.

Over the centuries and throughout most cultures and civilizations the family has been proven to be the unifying unit of society. Today we find the family under attack both from within and without. Outside forces would have us believe that the family as we have come to know and cherish it is no longer necessary. From within, the erosion of spiritual values and emphasis upon materialism has created for many families confusion and uncertainty where commitment and dedication once reigned. Marriage is holy. The home is sacred. Birth is a miracle. In these we find the very meaning of life itself.

Modern families are faced with many problems, but are these any greater than the problems overcome by the Holy Family? Joseph, the patient and loving husband desperately seeking a place for his devoted Mary to give birth to the holy child? The flight of the holy family into Egypt with their precious infant son to avoid persecution? The problems in raising this precocious youngster who was to become the Savior of the World? Parents the world over seek the best for their children. This is the very essence of universal human relations.

It is for these reasons that we pause to reflect, honor, and seek new ways and means of reinforcing the values and traditions that create devoted and loving families. To assist this noble effort in a more practical manner a list of suggestions is being offered for your consideration. [22]

An area of significant involvement of the archdiocese relating to family concerns is the service provided by it in aiding Greek-American couples to adopt children from Greece, a practice which began following World War II and the defeat of the Communists in Greece. This practice ended in 1973.

The record of the effort is documented in a series of encyclicals beginning in July 1959, when it was announced that the former, rather unorganized program for Greek adoptions was taking on a more orderly pattern with the designation of the archdiocese by the Greek government "for spiritual and moral reasons" as the sole responsible agent in the United States for these adoptions. The encyclical announced the establishment of an archdiocesan "Adoption Office."

Also related to the Church's concern for the family is the issue of divorce. The Orthodox Church does grant ecclesiastical divorces. There is, however, a pastoral concern with the ever-rising incidence of divorce in society as a whole. Priests are urged to do all in their power to limit this malaise of our society. For example, in a 1975 encyclical[24] priests are urged to preach on the subject frequently, to use personal pastoral contact wherever there are family problems, and to show concern early, before the problem becomes so serious as to cause thoughts of divorce. Previously, it was announced by encyclical that the priests would be required to offer "their conscientious, personal and professional opinion or judgment" in writing concerning divorce petitions, as well as verifying that they had "exercised their pastoral influence in each particular divorce case."[25]

Public Life

Archbishop Iakovos has consistently sought to relate his Church to the public life of the nation, issuing encyclicals on matters of national concern. He has led the way among Orthodox hierarchs in this country for involvement in the political process as well. Thus, in an Ochi Day encyclical in 1977, he directs the constituency of the Greek Orthodox Church to seek to influence the political leaders of the nation.

> As law-abiding citizens we also have the duty to defend the dignity of the nation in which we live by reminding our leaders to make decisions and take actions which would not undermine our nation's struggle for human rights or damage her prestige both here and abroad.[26]

Specific examples of involvement in the public life of the nation as illustrative of this pastoral concern are these: Assassination of President Kennedy, 1963; Prayer at Inauguration of President Nixon, 1973; Vietnam War Protest, 1975; Missing Persons in Cyprus, 1975; Camp David Summit Conference, 1978.[27] It is interesting to note the prophetic character of Archbishop Iakovos' prayer at the inauguration on January 20, 1973, of President Nixon and Vice President Agnew,

> who in *apparent* recognition of the awesome responsibilities, stand reverently before Thee. . . . Immerse their minds in the radiant spirit of Thy truth . . . their consciences in the purity of Thy sanctity. . . .For we wrestle, O Lord, not against flesh and blood, but against principalities, against powers, *against spiritual wickedness in high places. . .*[28] [emphasis mine].

Cyprus

It is not the place here to document or even to sketch out the remarkable story of the archdiocese's deep involvement in the Cyprus question. The wide-ranging concerns of the archdiocese, under the leadership of Archbishop Iakovos, include philanthropic concern for refugees and missing persons, appeals to human rights, appeal for the protection of the Ecumenical Patriarchate in Constantinople from Turkish oppression, the organization of what has come to be known on Capitol Hill as the "Greek Lobby," political pressure for an embargo on arms to Turkey, and unsuccessful efforts to sustain that embargo. It has included the organization of a strenuous fund-raising effort, telephone, letter, and telegram campaigns to sway Congressional subcommittees, individual senators and representatives in Congress, the State Department, the President of the United States, the U.N. General Assembly, and world public opinion. From the point of view of the Church, the justification for all this activity is summed up in a bitter encyclical following adverse action on the embargo in Congress:

The Cyprus question, which is clearly a humanitarian and moral imperative, has been turned into a political one. This has been done by political leaders who accept expediency as a basis for their actions, rather than rooting themselves in the self-evident truths, principles and traditions that made our Country the champion of all freedom-loving peoples throughout the world.

We, as Greek Orthodox communicants in America, bear the responsibility to carry the privileged burden of maintaining the spiritual and moral legacy of our forefathers. As descendants of a persecuted and martyred people, and as inheritors of the duty to defend the oppressed, we must protest the morally wrong position taken by our Administration and by a great number of Senators and Congressmen.

The 200,00 refugees and the 2,000 M.I.A.'s are such as a consequence of the breaking of the United Nations rule of law and can only be helped when U.N. Resolution 3212 is respected, and the slogan of human rights becomes a consistent policy of our foreign affairs. The Cyprus problem will be resolved when we openly trade for peace, rather than centering all our efforts on disarming peace by lifting an arms embargo.

In the spirit of love, justice, and reconciliation, you are instructed to write, or call our President and legislators to register your heartfelt concern for the rule of law in America and human rights in Cyprus.[29]

It should be emphasized that all this activity of the archbishop must be seen in the context not merely of ethnic interests but also of moral and spiritual obligation to those brethren who are unjustly treated. In an encyclical soliciting financial contributions for the Cypriot struggle, the archbishop defined the issue rightly:

> A few years ago we thought of ourselves only as Greek Americans and our own survival. . . . The Second World War . . . and the tragedy of Cyprus . . . broke our cage of isolation and they made us think of the survival of others. . . . We not only have our moral obligation . . . to help those unjustly treated: the persecuted, the uprooted and those being killed, but we must also condemn violence and injustice such as the "politics of expediency" which pays only lip service to moral principles.[30]

Philanthropies and Other Special Concerns

In the final entry on social-concern encyclicals, we find a wide variety of activities and interests on the part of Archbishop Iakovos and the Greek Orthodox Archdiocese.

Perhaps one of the most evident is Archbishop Iakovos' consistant concern with the support of the philanthropic institutions of the Ecumenical Patriarchate. Annually, in spite of a declining Greek Orthodox population in Constantinople, an appeal is made for a special collection in the churches of the archdiocese on the occasion of the feasts of the Unmercenary Saints Kosmas and Damian.[31] In the 1972 appeal, the archbishop mentioned some of the institutions supported by the patriarchate which the faithful in American were called upon to assist.

> Our Patriarch sponsors the children's camps on the islands of Proti and Pringipos near Constantinople, grants scholarships to poor students, provides dowries for poor brides, helps regularly the widows and orphans, and replenishes the funds of the Philoptochos of Constantinople in order to provide common meals in all the Greek schools there. [32]

However, concern for meeting human needs is not restricted to the patriarchal philanthropies. The archbishop also appeals to the faithful to assist those who suffer as a result of natural disasters. For example, appeals were sent for financial contributions to aid the 1970 typhoon victims in Pakistan. The archbishop referred to "our brethren in Pakistan" who were facing homelessness, hunger, disease, death, and other consequences of the typhoon. The archbishop instructed his flock that "it is our duty to come to the aid of those who suffered." For this purpose a special fund, "The Greek Archdiocese Pakistan Fund," was established and a collection in all churches was ordered for this purpose.[33]

Another appeal was for general support of those parishes which have suffered church-building fires. Thus, for example, appeals to all the churches were issued on behalf of churches in Pittsburg, California (1965),[34] Webster, Massachusetts (1966),[35] and the St. Eleftherios Church in New York City,[36] which had suffered fires. In addition, an appeal was made in 1977 to help in the restoration of the historic monastery of St. Catherine on Mt. Sinai following a disastrous fire in 1970.[37]

A number of encyclicals are devoted to questions dealing with youth. The concern of the Church for the young people of our age is admirably exemplified by this quotation from an encyclical on the occasion of the 1968 Observance of Archdiocese Youth Sunday, focusing on the drug abuse problem.

There was a time when the pitfalls of social evils would rarely attract young people of the Greek Orthodox Faith due to parental discipline and the high standards of home and family life. This immunity which was so long taken for granted has begun to erode. Some of our youth, and we are grateful to God that it is still a very small percentage, have been ensnared by various temptations of the secular life. We are especially concerned with the evil of drug addiction.

This disdainful temptation of the body destroys not only the flesh, but the God-given will of man as well. It violates every sacred concept of the mind, the soul and the body, and reduces the addict to a mere shell of the human form. The uncontrolled user of narcotics is further enslaved by the need to regularly replenish his supply, and in the fulfillment of this need further crime and debasement of his life often results.

We are, therefore, obliged to speak out with indignation and paternal remorse against this insidious evil which increasingly lures into its snare men and women of all ages and classes of society, but especially the young. Their broken lives are unimpeachable testimony of its vile and contemptible nature. I, therefore, urge that all of my reverend clergy, parish youth advisors and especially parents offer every cooperation and assistance to local service and government agencies concerned with its abatement and cure.

It is especially fitting, therefore, on this Archdiocese Youth Sunday of October 13, 1968, that we dedicate our prayers for the deliverance of those who have fallen victims to this temptation, and ask Almighty God to restore them in mind and body to the homes and broken hearts of those who love them and pray for their recovery.[38]

To be sure, the archbishop issued encyclicals focusing on youth, its problems, and efforts to strengthen the ties of young people with the Church and to build up their spiritual and moral founda- tions.[39] Included in this concern are the highly successful youth camps throughout the archdiocese, and most importantly the Arch- diocesan Camp Program in Greece based in the archdiocese-owned camp known as Ionian Village, which serves youth from high school to college age.

A concern for traffic safety has consistently been one of the emphases of the archbishop. Encyclicals have been issued annually on Labor Day in support of the National Safety Council campaigns to reduce traffic accident fatalities. In a 1963 directive to priests the archbishop highlights the issue in moral and spiritual terms:

I am, therefore, urging you to impress upon our faithful com- municants in the church the vital necessity for exercising safety in all forms and at all times. Towards this end, and at the re- quest of the National Safety Council, I am asking you to read this Pastoral Letter in Church to your congregation after ser- vices on Sunday, September 1 of this year, the day before Labor Day during the summer season's last weekend when many unnecessary accidents occur, and again on Sunday, Sep- tember 8, near the time when our children are returning to school and to add thereto your own heartfelt remarks on this most momentous and disaster-fraught subject.

On this occasion you should stress the compelling need for exercising safety in all forms and especially on our streets and highways, either as drivers or pedestrians, or passengers of a motor vehicle, or as participants in any form of transportation, clearly pointing out, as befits the spiritual leader, the moral and sacred responsibility all of us have to avoid that undue negli- gence leading to unnecessary death and injury which consti- tutes in a very real sense godlessness and sin against mankind.[40]

A whole series of encyclicals witness this concern for the safety of the citizenry.[41]

Another area of concern is with the blind. Frequent appeals for assistance to the blind, especially in Greece, have been made; some on behalf of agencies, such as the "American Friends for the Blind in Greece."[42]

Many other topics of social concern have been the subject of

Archbishop Iakovos' encyclicals during the twenty years of his archepiscopal leadership of the Greek Orthodox Church in the Americas. Among these concerns are racism,[43] pollution,[44] the hospitalized,[45] dowries for poor Greek girls,[46] road-building equipment for Greece,[47] Greek citizens hospitalized in Greece,[48] Greek "Junior Leagues" for service to orphaned children,[49] handicapped artists,[50] support for the Red Cross,[51] and Cooley's anemia,[52] a hereditary illness of the blood found in high incidence among Greek Orthodox people. Associated with the general concern with social issues was the announcement in 1971 of the establishment of the Archdiocesan Social Health and Welfare Center, with two offices, one at the archdiocesan headquarters and the other on Long Island. According to the archbishop, the center's purpose was to provide adequate guidance and assistance "to Greek Orthodox Communicants in the areas of welfare, health and social needs." More particularly, it was indicated that the center was to serve "the ever-increasing needs of new immigrants from Greece, aid victims of drug addiction, assist those in need of welfare guidance and make legal counsel available to those who need it."[53]

*   *   *   *   *

Though this survey of the encyclicals issued during the twenty-year period of the primacy of Archbishop Iakovos is far from complete, the evidence gathered indicates a consistent and wide-ranging concern with those aspects of Orthodox Christian life that deal with moral and social issues. Inspiring this concern, it appears, is a belief in Orthodox Christianity not only as a faith of traditions and doctrine, but primarily as a living and vital faith. Reflecting this attitude, this study will close with some excerpts from a sermon by His Eminence Archbishop Iakovos entitled: "Is Orthodoxy a Faith or a Commitment?", preached at a Pan-Orthodox vesper service in 1974:

It is high time that the Orthodox Christians in America rise to the demands of the time, look ahead and endeavor to respond to the unanswered questions of a whole generation . . . here in the United States, from professorial chairs and from pulpit to declare the militant and the prophetic character of Orthodoxy. But as a Church, we have failed, and lamentably so, to either prove it or to live it in a fearless and deeply conscientious manner.

The hour of Orthodoxy, my friends, is not tommorrow. It is

NOW! For Orthodoxy as we proclaim it in the morning service and again this evening, presents us and the world with a challenge to live Christianity with a glad and vibrant heart; and thus proclaim it as the only inspiring and creative and saving faith. Orthodoxy is an overflowing fountainhead from which all Christians can draw and quench the thirst of their souls. Orthodoxy belongs to all, as Christianity and truth and God belong to all.

If Orthodoxy is being characterized as a liturgical faith, and it is so, it is because Orthodoxy believes that it is a religion at the service of the people, rallying the poeple and moving the people, and leading the people forward, not only in moments of danger or distress, but also in times of prosperity and peace. For Liturgy has always been the very soul and conscience of Orthodox Christianity.

Liturgical processions in the Orthodox tradition are manifestations of the spiritual impact which their belief in the living God exerts upon their lives. Orthodoxy is not a casual or an occasional religious experience. It responds to a Christian's day-to-day existence and to all of his aspirations and needs, which are prompted either by relations, or by nature itself.[54]

NOTES

1. Charles E. Fager, *Selma, 1965* (New York, 1974), p. 134. See also, photograph no. 22, between pages 178 and 179.

2. See my article "The Local Church: An Eastern Orthodox Perspective." *The Ecumenical Review*, 29 (1977), pp. 141-53.

3. Demetrios J. Constantelos, *Encyclicals and Documents of the Greek Orthodox Archdiocese of North and South America* (Thessalonike, 1976), p. 1266.

4. Ibid., Table of Contents, pp. 15-16.

5. I wish to acknowledge my gratitude to His Eminence Archbishop Iakovos for permission to consult the Archives and the assistance of Rev. Methodios Tournas and Miss Nike Kale, secretary to Archbishop Iakovos, in researching the encyclicals of this period.

6. The nature of the encyclical as a popular teaching medium does not call for detailed, documented and scholarly justification. As a means for instructing the flock, it is, rather kerygmatic in character, vocative in style and authoritative in ethos. All references, therefore, tend to be short emphases in short communications which rarely go beyond three pages in length and which more normally are limited to a single page.

7. Examples from quite varying trends in the Orthodox Church of Greece are: Christian Union of Professional Men of Greece, *Towards a Christian Civilization* (Athens, 1950); P. Melites (Alexandros Tsirintanes), *Gia na anoixe ho dromos* (Athens, 1957); Panagiotes Demetropoulos, *Orthodoxos Christianike Ethike* (Athens, 1970); Christos Giannaras, *He elevtheria tou ethous* (Athens, 1970); Georgios Mantzarides, "The Witness of Orthodoxy to the Contemporary World," *St. Vladimir's Theological Quarterly* 17 (1973), pp. 170-80.

8. Archives. Protocol No. 157.

9. See Constantelos, *Encyclicals* pp. 1165-66; and Archives, Protocol Nos. 215; 194, 215, 105, 107.

10. Constantelos, *Encyclicals*, pp. 1225-28.

11. Ibid., pp. 1086-88; No. 25, pp. 1156-59; No. 237, p. 1040; No. 175, p. 1134; and Archives. Protocol nos. 45, 200, 11, 50, 98.

12. Ibid., Protocol No. 50.

13. Ibid., Nov. 19, 1978. Protocol No. 170.

14. Constantelos, Protocol no. 237 and News release, Nov. 12, 1964, pp. 1040-44.

15. Ibid., April 21, 1965, pp. 1183-85.

16. Archives, News release, July 17, 1978.

17. Constantelos, Protocol No. 33, pp. 1242-45.

18. Ibid., March 25, 1977. Protocol No. 39.

19. Ibid., Protocol No. 15.

20. Ibid., Oct. 22, 1979, Protocol No. 237, pp. 1161-62.

21. Ibid., May 4, 1975, no Protocol No.

22. Ibid., May 1, 1972, Protocol No. 44, pp. 1072-77.

23. Ibid., July 1, 1959, no Protocol No., pp. 1018-19.

24. Ibid., Sept. 24, 1975, no Protocol No.

25. Ibid., Nov. 21, 1973, Protocol No. 206A.

26. Ibid., Oct. 28, 1977, Protocol No. 207.

27. Ibid., Nov. 23, 1963, pp. 1162-63. Texts of telegrams, pp. 1163-65; See also archives, News release, Jan. 20, 1973; News release, "Archbishop Iakovos Responds to President Ford and Vice President Rockefeller's Statements," April 25, 1975, ibid., News release, July 2, 1975, telegrams to U.S. President and officials on the 2500 missing persons in Cyprus, ibid.; and News release, Sept. 7, 1978, "Archbishop Iakovos sends telegrams to President Carter, President Sadat, and Prime Minister Begin," ibid.

28. My emphasis, Archives, 1973.

29. Archives, June 20, 1978, no Protocol No. For a list of encyclicals dealing with the Cyprus issue, see Constantelos, pp. 1167-70, 1173-74, 1040, and 1150-1255.

30. Archives, Aug. 28, 1974, Protocol. No. 74.

31. Constantelos, Oct. 11, 1960, pp. 1021-22; Oct. 11, 1961, pp. 1029-30; Jan. 3, 1961, pp. 1023-24; Sept. 18, 1962, p. 1033; Sept. 24, 1963, pp. 1034-36; Sept. 4, 1971, pp. 1069-70; Sept. 14, 1972, pp. 1077-88; Archives Sept. 10, 1973; Oct. 21, 1974, Sept. 26, 1975; Oct. 12, 1976; Oct. 12, 1977, and Oct. 4, 1978.

32. Ibid.

33. Ibid., Dec. 1, 1970, pp. 1065-66. Similar appeals for various other causes in ibid., pp. 1038-39, 1044-45, and 1047-48.

34. Ibid., Aug. 12, 1965, pp. 1045-47.

35. Ibid., March 30, 1966, pp. 1049-50.

36. Archives, Aug. 21, 1973.

37. Ibid., Nov. 27, 1977.

38. Constantelos, Oct. 7, 1968, p. 1085.

39. Ibid., pp. 1053-54, 1080-81, and 1089.

40. Ibid., Aug. 1, 1963, pp. 1159-60.

41. Labor Day encyclicals on traffic safety can be found in ibid., Aug. 23, 1961, pp. 1151-52; Sept. 1, 1964, pp. 1070-71; Aug. 25, 1969, pp. 1233-34; and Archives, Aug. 24, 1973, Sept. 11, 1977.

42. See encyclicals such as that of May 14, 1961 in ibid., pp. 1027-28; May 18, 1964, p. 1039; May 7, 1969.

43. Ibid., March 16, 1965, p. 1181.

44. Ibid., Nov. 7, 1971, pp. 1086-88.

45. Ibid., April 21, 1959, p. 1017.

46. Ibid., May 24, 1960, pp. 1019-20.

47. Ibid., May 9, 1961, p. 1027.

48. Ibid., May 15, 1961. pp. 1028-29.

49. Ibid., No date, p. 1031-32.

50. Ibid., Nov. 13, 1963, pp. 1036-37.

51. Ibid., Jan. 14, 1970, pp. 1064-65.

52. Ibid., Nov. 28, 1972, pp. 1078-79 and Archives, April, 1973.

53. Constantelos, *Encyclicals*, News release, pp. 1071. The announcement of the office was issued in Greek on September 29, 1971, Archives, news release.

54. "An Address delivered by His Eminence Archbishop Iakovos following a Pan-Orthodox Vespers in Holy Trinity Serbian Orthodox Church in Pittsburgh on the Sunday of Orthodoxy, March 3, hosted by the Orthodoxy Clergy Fellowship of Greater Pittsburgh." This release is included in the Archdiocesan Archives of encyclicals for the year 1974. The document itself bears no notice of the year in which the sermon was preached.

Chapter Three

SOCIAL CONCERN IN THE CLERGY-LAITY
CONGRESS KEYNOTE ADDRESSES

Every two years, according to the charter and bylaws of the Greek Orthodox Archdiocese of North and South America, a clergy-laity congress is held. The purpose of these congresses is to deal with the administrative affairs of the church. Specifically excluded from its formal concerns and legislative authority are questions of faith and doctrine. Yet, as the church gathers together in these biennial occasions, it is difficult, if not impossible, to isolate the mundane administrative concerns of the Archdiocese from the demands of faith. What was once a basically functional working and social meeting, is in the process of slowly being transformed into a more spiritually oriented and more representative agency for the full range of the concerns of faith. An example of such a change is to be seen in the Committee on Finances which traditionally attracts the largest number of participants. An ever-increasing concern for truly Christian motivated giving has transformed this committee over the years. Once firmly grounded in a head-tax, assessment mentality, it has, over the years, become a strong force in the development of a spiritually grounded stewardship program of fund-raising for the church. [1]

A chief source for this development is the spirit and focus imparted by the 'keynote' addresses of Archbishop Iakovos at the inauguration of the congresses. These keynote addresses have provided a platform for the church's primate to assess the direction and development of the church, to guide the future orientation of the church, and to articulate hopes and dreams. Though often—as is to be expected—the keynote addresses deal with on-going 'in-house' interests of the parish life of the church and with the demands placed upon the Archdiocese as the administrative and organizational center of the Church, more and more, these addresses cast that concern in the context of the Orthodox Christian faith and its demand that all expressions of the church's life reflect it. One concern addressed in such keynote remarks is the philanthropic and social outreach of the church, as distinguished from the organizational, financial, legislative, and cultural interests of the church. In these pages we will survey the keynote addresses of the ten clergy-laity congresses held during the twenty year period of the hierarchical tenure of Archbishop Iakovos, 1960-1980.

The Fifteenth Clergy-Laity Congress

The Fifteenth Clergy-Laity Congress of the Greek Orthodox Archdiocese of North and South America was held in 1960 in Buffalo, New York. Most of the topics included in the keynote address dealt with the routine administrative concerns and competency of the congress. Of special interest to us in this study on social concern in the Archdiocese, however, is a section of the address on philanthropy. There the Archbishop said:

Philanthropy is another area of activity for our church, and for our Archdiocese, an area which is usually without any workers. The only time we run and fill its ranks is when either we ourselves or some of our own people are struck by some misfortune, such as, for example, the earthquakes in recent years in the Ionian Islands and Thessalia. When, however, an earthquake strikes a nation such as Chile in South America, in which we ourselves have three parishes, then the Archdiocese is restricted to a telegram of sympathy, unable to offer anything more substantial . . . Unfortunately we fold our hands, our empty hands, and we hear the bitter comments from those who come to us "What is the Archdiocese doing?" The Archdiocese has to have a philanthropic fund. Today we commit only a symbolic amount in our budget for philanthropic purposes . . . But the Archdiocese is all of us. Are we ready to examine ourselves on this question? Are we prepared to conduct an investigation which doubtlessly would have as a consequence that we would assume greater responsibilities in reference to the Archdiocesan philanthropies program? As Archbishop I pray for it and call for it. [2]

This address in 1960 also included references in support of the Patriarchate which were defined as "responsibilities which are in the first instance moral and spiritual and only subsequently financial." [3] Most of the other topics, in this first keynote address of the then new Archbishop dealt with issues of internal organization. Yet, the challenge to philanthropy in this context is all the more to be noticed and highlighted.

The Sixteenth Clergy-Laity Congress

The Sixteenth Clergy-Laity Congress was held in Boston in 1962. The message of His Eminence Archbishop Iakovos was delivered to the congress on Monday, 25 June 1962. It was a long address of thirty-eight closely typewritten pages with exclusive focus on the inner life of the parishes and Archdiocese.[4] It exemplified a strong sense of purpose and leadership on the part of the Archbishop. Though nothing in the message can be clearly designated as specifically related to social concerns, two emphases were to lay the foundations for the involvement of subsequent congresses in social concerns. In the first instance, there was a strong effort on the part of the Archbishop to move the atmosphere of the congress—and as a consequence, the relations of the parishes with the Archdiocese—to a more spiritually grounded orientation. Though nearly the whole agenda of the congress dealt with administrative, financial, and cultural concerns, the Archbishop began his address on a completely different note.

If we do not feel the presence of the Lord and we do not hear within us this prayer of Jesus every single day of this conclave, this will denote that the congress does not have a sacred purpose and that it is not going to fulfill any spiritual goal. Moreover, if we fail to hear the words of Jesus in our hearts, it follows that we have not been able to comprehend nor to be moved by the prayer of His All Holiness our Ecumenical Patriarch 'that we progress in every good effort pleasing unto God and that we grow ever stronger.'

I want to abide in the hope, however, that we shall experience the presence of the Lord in our midst and that we shall always hear the warm resounding voice of our Holy Father and Patriarch so that day by day we may progress and increase in the faith.

This can become one of the most discouraging meetings ever held, if each of us does not particpate in the Congress with the fullest expression of the reflections of his soul and conscience. If the word of God, the truth, and the strongest possible expression of our Christian duty do not serve as the basic criteria of our decisions at this congress, then we will have failed. This must not become a convention of the type in which rationalizations dominate the discussion and decisions are considered to be the result of a "voice-vote." Our decisions should be reached after due consideration of our common obligation to the truth, to Christ, and to the Church.[5]

The second foundational emphasis was unity. The motto of the congress was "that we may all be one." Its major emphasis in the address was not ecumenical. Rather, it called for the unity of the parishes under the central direction of the Archdiocese and the unity of the parishioners in their parishes. Throughout the address the emphasis was on the unity of the parishes under the leadership of the Archdiocese. The chief vehicle for the unity was seen to be the adoption of the *Constitution and Uniform Regulations* of the Archdiocese by the local parishes. Thus, in the review of the activities and work of the local bishops, a central feature was a public recital of the number of parishes in each District which has and had not approved the *Constitution and Uniform Regulations.* The rationale was forthrightly set out: "All existing signs point to one thing: that all our communities shall soon adopt it, because it exists for their benefit. It exists for them and was set forth by them. Our communities and community leaders now believe that only with a uniform consitution can we create a spirit of peaceful progress, and a promising future." [6]

The same was true for the emphasis on the unity of the local parish. The Archbishop thus emphasized:

It is necessary that the Greek Orthodox Community be based continually on the principle of unity of heart and soul; her essence must be derived from having 'all in common' and not on simply interests; her center or nucleus and periphery must be the Resurrection, i.e., the intent to live, function, and prosper in the Resurrection. In other words, for the resurrecting of the ethically and morally fallen souls, for the birth and revivification of the spiritually dead, and especially to make the resurrection the desire, ideal, and conscientious aspiration of all its members." [7]

Spiritual renewal and focus, coupled with unity of the faithful in the parishes and the unity of the parishes in the Archdiocese, were the two foundations for the future development of the church. Though the bulk of the address dealt with a review of the progress of the preceding two years (bishops, archdiocesan institutions, archdiocese activities, community building programs and projects, the church's position as a major faith), the thrust of the message was that renewed spiritual life and the unity of the faithful under the Archdiocese would provide the momentum for forward movement and progress. Thus, early in the talk (p. 3), these words of vision could be found: "Our Community must not be merely a place for one to meet—but rather a place where one may meet for a common drive forward; a drive toward moral and spiritual perfection." Near the conclusion of the address there was a challenge to the parish leaders assembled to grow, to reach out, to assume responsibility, and above all to progress.

This is the image of our church today. Orthodoxy is constantly growing as a faith and as a way of life, as a tradition and a heritage, as a church and a mission. As we recognize this fact, we are obliged to assume certain responsibilities which we cannot and must not avoid. On the contrary, we must rise to the occasion and fulfill these responsibilities, even if for some this will necessitate personal sacrifices. Lest we forget, both our church and our nation were established with sacrifices.

Our first obligation is to seek progress. If our country were to ever take another name, that name would be Progress. No other country bears this mark so clearly. In our land, progress is the primary consideration, no sacrifice is too great for the sake of progress. The United States is the only country in which new roads are being opened constantly. This is the only country in which work is conducted around the clock; the only country which is constantly moving forward on land and in space.

Our first obligation as a church, therefore, is to seek progress. We must move forward in construction and administration, in spiritual and moral achievement, in degree and content. Our church must expand the horizon of its vision in all directions. The church must emerge from the barriers erected by community isolationalists in order to face the challenge on an ecumenical plane. [8]

The challenge to progress was dramatically emphasized with the last charge of the Archbishop to the church: "Our final responsibility as a church is to reach for the stars. To believe in the unbelievable and to labor for the seemingly impossible goals. [9] It is this forward-reaching spirit which was to characterize the Archdiocese for the balance of the first twenty years, including a forward movement into the areas of social concern.

The Seventeenth Clergy-Laity Congress

The new direction promised in the Archbishop's address of the Boston Congress began to unfold in the keynote address of the Seventeenth Clergy-Laity Congress held in Denver, Colorado in 1964. Significantly titled "Prelude," [10] it carried as a text the following biblical passage: "Blessed be the God and Father of our Lord Jesus Christ! By His great mercy we have been born anew to a living hope, to an inheritance which is imperishable, undefiled and unfading" (1 Pet. 1.3-4). The text of the message of the Archbishop seems to have been chosen as a bridge between the preceding congress and the Denver Congress. The call to spiritual renewal and unity, which concluded in an affirmation of the idea of progress in the former congress, now began to sketch out the lines of hope and ecclesial rebirth.

The report began with a historical overview of the Greek Orthodox presence in the Americas, beginning with the New Smyrna Settlement of 1767. It focused secondly on the purchase in 1867 of the land for the first Greek Orthodox church in America in New Orleans. Thirdly, it looked forward to the immediately forthcoming date of 1967, as the beginning of the third century of Greek Orthodox presence in this country. Of this new century the Archbishop wrote: "Today we are not faced with the need of marking a new road. This new road for us was marked in 1767; it was opened fully in 1867; and it must become a highway in 1967."[11] It was on this note of positive expectation and hope that the Denver Congress began.

The emphasis on spiritual orientation for the work of the Church was restated with the obvious corollary of responsibility:

Our Church is not simply an organization: it is the Body of Christ! Regrettably it is seldom conceived by us in this manner. If we could realize that the Church is the Body of Christ, then, we as true Christians, would seek our responsible place within this Body. . . . The familiar phrase, 'I am a member of the community,' must be supplanted within our conscience by the more appropriate phrase, 'I am a member of the Body,' in order that the Body may live eternally, and have as its purpose, our salvation.[12]

The meaning of this commitment was then delineated. It meant that the church's mission was to share the faith and to permit the light of Orthodoxy to shine forth. It meant that the Archbishop was calling his church to cease thinking of itself as a passing visitor to the American scene and to assume a stance of involvement in the life of the nation.

Our church in America can no longer remain merely a spectator and listener, nor can it be satisfied with the role of a complainer.

No one in America, truly driven by ambition to work, and improve himself and thus project his own identity, can be ignored. Our church must remove itself from the sidelines and place itself fully in the center of American life. It must labor and struggle to develop its spiritual life and thus assume its place among the other churches as a living, thriving, courageous church ready to accept responsibilities and eager to submit to sacrifice. [13]

This forward-looking mission meant for the Archbishop a new set of priorities, which significantly for this study, included a strong emphasis on issues of social concern.

Our church cannot go forward as long as it continues to look backward. As the church of the future, we can no longer permit ourselves to discuss subjects concerning membership dues, parish boundaries, uniform bylaws, election irregularities and matters of local interest. A church of the future must concern itself with the fundamental problems of divorce, marriages not blessed by the Church, baptisms which have never been performed, a diluted Orthodox consciousness, pantheistic or pan-religious syncretism, nominal Orthodoxy, secular spirit, corruption of morals, hoodlumism, juvenile crime, and in general, reform of its constituency. [14]

Under the rubric, "The Demands of the Times," the Archbishop responded: "Works." His focus included concerns pertinent to inner life and functioning of the church: constitution, priests, religious education, Greek education, discipline and laity. But there were outreach concerns as well, such as public relations and interchurch relations. However, social concerns were not absent. There was a paragraph on the family and the problems of divorce, [15] the organization of a philanthropic agency, and youth work. Significant was a call at this Congress of 1964 for "an organization to coordinate the power of the Greek-American voter." The Archbishop opined: "I believe that the existence of such an organization is essential, because as Americans we are obliged to assume a position on many political and social issues. This we cannot and should not do as a church, because our church believes fully in the principles of the separation of church and state." [16] This appears to be one of the earliest calls for involvement in the political processes of our nation by the Greek Orthodox Church for purposes of social concern. It was not to be realized until the Cyprus conflict a decade later. But the Archbishop had set the course.

The Eighteenth Clergy-Laity Congress

For the first time in the history of the Greek Orthodox Archdiocese of North and South America, a clergy-laity congress, the
eighteenth, was held in Canada. In 1966, this meeting of the church
was to prove historical in another sense as well. It was the first
clergy-laity congress to have a working committee on "Social and
Moral Issues," as we shall see in the chapter which follows. Not un-
reatedly. Archbishop Iakovos' keynote address[17] had several
significant references to social concerns. The message was short—
only ten typewritten pages. Familiar themes were repeated in new
and fresh words.

> In our zeal to see our church more firmly established in the
> second century, and in our dreams of seeing it a living and
> triumphant and major faith that is exercising a dominant
> spiritual and moral influence, let us not permit ourselves even
> for a moment to rest on what we have been in the past. On the
> contrary, what we must do for ourselves and for our church is
> to renew ourselves constantly, becoming "conformed to the
> image of His Son" (Rom. 8.29), and living the life of our Church,
> her oneness, her holiness, her catholicity, her apostolicity con-
> scientiously and in all their fullness. [18]

A call to a "new and more robust life, full of vigor, full of creative-
ness," to a "revolution within us," to "self-criticism," to "awak-
ening sobriety and renewal," to "vigilance and spiritual aggressive-
ness," to "unity and union" in an ecumenical, ecclesial, and personal context summarized the themes of past keynote addresses
and deepened their understanding for the church. In conjunction
with these themes, several ethical and moral topics were dealt
with. Early in the address, for instance, the Archbishop criticized
the separation by some "theologians, clerics and laymen" of faith
and science while concurrently warning the world "not to succumb
to the temptation of omnipotence, omnipresence, and omniscience
which our preeminently scientific and technological age puts before us."[19] In addition, he called the Church to "a century of rebuilding and reordering Christian moral and spiritual principles
and values" and encouraged his flock to "see in particular how it
might be possible for us to contribute so that the twentieth century
. . . could become . . . a century of rebuilding and reordering
Christian moral and spiritual principles and values." [20]

A major theme of the address is ecumenism. It is at once an
existential analysis of Orthodox attitudes, theological positions,

and a history of involvement. In addition, it tended to focus on the "life and work" dimension of ecumenical activity with a significant emphasis on issues of worldwide social concern. The whole passage deserves quoting:

We desire unity. It will be the seal of our faith in Christ Jesus. Nor are we afraid of union, for we prefer to see "a Christendom arching freely over seas and continents, one and unique in its substance, one end united in its mission to the world, and one common confrontation of its problems. . ." as His Holiness the Ecumenical Patriarch wrote in his paschal encyclical this year. And the problems that need to be faced in common by all of us united are these: 1) the problem of overpopulation of the earth and the issue of birth control, 2) the problem of hunger affecting millions of people, 3) the problem of world health, 4) the problem of total disarmament, 5) the problem of the arms race, 6) the problem of the cold war, 7) the problem of social equality, 8) the problem of freedom of conscience, 9) the problem of underdeveloped peoples, 10) the problem of atheism, 11) the problem of the religious crisis, 12) the problem of communism, and 13) the problem of relations with other religions.[21]

A second major theme of this address is entitled: "Restructuring and Reordering of Spiritual and Moral Principles and Values." The Archbishop analyzes the moral climate and finds that a "terrible confusion and inversion and distortion has been suffered by those spiritual and moral principles and values which for ages were used as guidelines and as the basis for forming and developing human character."[22] But there is more than analysis and critique, for the address notes, "the work of the Church is not to diagnose a symptom but to heal the affliction no matter how long it takes, no matter how great the pain or the cost."[23] And once again, the Archbishop brought before the members of his church a new litany, a litany of moral and social concerns for them to deal with as a church and as God's people.

This is not a sermon. It is the overture of a symphony, the most beautiful of all—the symphony, the harmony between faith and practice.

And this overture must first resound in our conscience, secondly in our homes, thirdly in our parish halls, and finally from the rooftops of our houses. For no problem affecting our nation, the world, of our fellow man, can find us indifferent.

Neither the problem of the 'new morality' which is without

moral basis; nor the problem of youth, unprotected and exposed to every danger; nor the problem of the intellectual and moral well-being of the members of our parishes; nor the problem of the total secularization of the Christian family, nor the problem of divorce which threatens to destroy the foundation of marriage; nor the problem of crying social and economic inequality among people; nor the problem of political immunity of the unscrupulous leaders of the world; nor the problem of war, hot or cold, or the war of nerves; nor the problem of the world's population explosion and the effect it is likely to have on the social order; nor the problem of hypocritical conservatism or insolent liberalism.

Pindar proclaimed, 'When we begin a work we must place in the forefront a man of radiant countenance.' And this proclamation of our second century, and of the new work of our church which commences with it, cannot be other than the beginning of a new orientation, a new start, a new spiritual and moral mobilization. Let us give our full attention to that admonition of Saint Peter which has never been so timely: ". . . supplement your faith with virtue . . . brotherly affection with love" (2 Pet. 1.5-8).[24]

This address is a turning point for the area of social concern in the Orthodox Church in this country. The Eighteenth Clergy-Laity Congress will be recorded in history as the point in time in which Orthodox Christianity made a turn from introspection and exclusive self-concern to viewing itself as responsible for the moral and social concerns of the age. It would take a long process to flesh out that new concern—a process still incomplete—but Montreal may be remembered for the discipline of social ethics, in truth as "the beginning of a new orientation, a new start, a new spiritual and moral orientation."[25] The appeal in the peroration of this address summed it up well: "Rise far above yourselves. See the new image of our church, and desire a greater role of our church on all matters, local, national, and worldwide, so long as these touch upon the work and mission of our church."[26]

The Nineteenth Clergy-Laity Congress

Athens, Greece, was the location of the Nineteenth Clergy-Laity Congress held from July 20-27, 1968. The proceedings of the congress were published in an impressive book.[27] Included in it was the address by His Eminence Archbishop Iakovos.[28] The theme of the congress and of the message was the Pauline verse "Of one accord, of one mind" (Phil. 2.2), focusing the continuing theme of unity in the relations between the Greek Orthodox Church in the Americas and the Orthodox of Greece. The address spoke to the latter; it sought to explain the American church to the people in Greece. Striking at tendencies to view the Greek-Americans as an ethnic colony of Greece, the Archbishop demolished the notion.

We, the Greeks of America, are first and foremost a church. If you regard us as immigrants, you have committed your first error.

Our parishes began as organizations and developed into religious communities. Today, they are churches.[29]

There is the desire that the bond between Greece and the Greek-Americans be kept strong so that they be "of one accord" and "of one mind," but on new terms. It is with a certain sense of autonomy that the Church of America presented itself to the people of Greece at this clergy-laity congress—a sure sign of its own maturation.

In reading the text, it is clear that it seeks to present the Archdiocese in an honest way to the Greek public. Yet, it still serves, in the hands of Archbishop Iakovos, in a tangible yet significant way, to raise up issues of social concern. Presenting the search for the unity of the Greek Orthodox Church in America as the "principal pursuit," the Archbishop presented a description of the social and moral climate of the times, as an illustration of the difficulty of the task. It was a perceptive socio-ethical analysis.

Our essential stand, however, is one along a united front: resolute, 'of one accord,' without defections or desertions. If we are possessed by agony, it is because we live in a time of great upheavals affecting the intellectual, philosophical and theological outlooks on life. If we feel distress in our heart, it is because we are witnesses to radical re-classification of values. Much time will elapse before a re-classification of new values is effected—if such will ever be. At this moment, however, our values are undergoing an earthquake threatening them with total collapse. The first cracks appear as the discarding of all accepted spiritual and ethical values, and result in either a confused philosophy of eudaimonism and cynicism, or in a contradictory co-existence of existentialism and nihilism.

Today's political, economic, social, and spiritual climate in America is not at all conducive to favoring the normal develop-

ment and shaping of the mind and the ethos of the average man.
This observation attests to that distress of heart to which I
referred earlier. And it is just that distress of the heart which we
feel at this moment. Everything—religion, language, family
tradition, ethnic heritage—is under judgment. All these are accepted values, and all these are being overturned. [30]

In the concluding summary of the address, there was another
similar analysis especially perceptive of the moral climate of
America in the late sixties and early seventies. Presented with a
certain kerygmatic passion it, nevertheless, provided deep insight
to the social problems of the day. I quote the passage extensively.

As you well know, we live today in a period without precedence
in the history of America. Cynicism is rampant and everything
that is traditional is challenged and rejected.

Where we once had real values, we now have empty words.
What was respect for man, is now the shameful exploitation
of him. Liberty has been replaced by a merciless slavery, which
is spiritual and moral slavery. Justice has become injustice. The
dignity of man has given way to the maltreatment of man. Friend-
ship turns into revengeful hatred; self-confidence into moral
bankruptcy; respect for law into lawless rebellion; modesty into
insolence; academic freedom into anarchy by students; the right-
eous outcry into hypocritical slogans; truth into the ugliest lie;
the helpful dialectic into slanderous preachings; technology into
technocracy; beautiful art into ugliness; purity into the worst
vulgarity.

Within these twistings of values, logic becomes irrational, justice
is strangled, truth is distorted, prudence is disregarded, religion
is reduced to a meaningless or a sadistical discussion in which all
we held sacred is reviled. It is in such a world that modern man
and his church must live. [31]

How is this situation to be faced? The Archbishop exhorts that
for the Orthodox Christian to face this reality effectively it is
necessary to perceive his faith as directly applicable to the problems of the age. Thus he opines:

It is necessary that Orthodoxy be vividly and dynamically
interpreted as a theology or a correct way of life for the present-day Greek Orthodox, in a language and terminology which
will meet the spiritual and moral needs of our times. Orthodoxy
as a faith, as a theology, as a worship, as a tradition, and as a

satisfying and a salutary power must never become a stylized form, but it must increasingly become an inseparable element and dynamic part of our life. [32]

It is, of course, not only the task of theological interpretation to make the influence of the Church felt on social concerns, but the archepiscopal guidelines presented here are sufficient warrant for continued and intensified theological study of the Orthodox Christian foundations for social ethics.

In the area of practical effort and action the message ascribed to priests a leadership role in philanthropy, [33] called for the co-operation and leadership of the Church of Greece "as the only truly free Orthodox Church," [34] and underlined the concern of the Church in America for the youth and family life. [35] Further, in response to the crises of the age, the Archbishop presented the Orthodox of America as actively responding: "Those of us who are in America, knowing that we face a crisis that tries our conscience, attempt to react in a way that will not allow us to avoid taking a definite stand; and we try to take a stand that is consistent with the will of God." [36]

Concretely expressed, the Office of Inter-Church Relations is described in this message as exercising such a role in an ecumenical context, though the Archbishop concurrently rejects Greek-American involvement in the national politics of Greece and any church involvement in American partisan politics. [37] Regarding the activities of the Office of Inter-Church Relations, he said:

Through this office, we express our opposition to certain positions taken by churches or religious organizations in certain areas, such as the questions of prayer and the reading of the Bible in the public schools of America, or when they assume extreme positions on ethical, social, economic, political or international questions. The position of our church is only expressed after long, detailed, and responsible consideration of such subjects. We are, of course, very much concerned with injustice, or prejudice, or victims of unfair laws, but we do not allow emotionalism to decisively affect our position. We believe that in such circumstances, prudence, moderation and objectivity are more fitting characteristics of a church with authority and Christian responsibility. [38]

The Twentieth Clergy-Laity Congress

New York City was the location of the Twentieth Clergy-

Laity Congress of the Greek Orthodox Archdiocese, held in 1970.
The keynote address of His Eminence Archbishop Iakovos was appropriately entitled: "Toward the Decade 1970-1980."[39] The
style, it needs to be noted, of this address was quite different from
all those which preceded it. Whereas the former were clearly cast
in kerygmatic style, addressed to the hearts as well as the minds of
the listeners and readers, written with a certain literary flair, the
address to the Twentieth Clergy-Laity Congress bore none of these
characteristics. It was formed, 'objectively,' 'intellectually,' and in
some fashion 'detached.' It ultimately was to become one of the
most controversial speeches of the tenure of Archbishop Iakovos
because of proposals regarding the use of English by the church.
Though notes of hope and enthusiasm are not lacking, its pessimistic
tone was out of character with the addresses which both preceded
and followed it.

The structure of the address included the following major topical
divisions: "Our Church Today" and "Our Congress Topics." The
"Assessment of the Status of the Church" in 1970 began with a
survey of opinions in the church about that which guaranteed its
liveliness and growth. This is followed by three suggested areas of
general improvement for the church. The leading two of these
areas, i.e. the church as co-workers with God, and the image of
the church as spiritual, lead to the third which included, among its
concerns, social involvement.

Thus, the Archbishop spoke of the "acts, conversations and
general deportment of many of us [as] characterized by such de-
cadence that it can only contribute to the increased deterioration
of morality in our society. " When he proceeded to discuss "the
area of social involvement and action," the same realism and negative assessment prevailed, though this became an occasion to
demand much more of his flock.

The pulpit is utilized on numerous occasions to refer to social
subjects, without basing our reference on Orthodox ethical
or theological positions, which would make our sermon an important lesson in religious education.

Let us now come to the area of social involvement and action.
Such action is generally limited among our people. Only spora-
dically are we concerned, and then mainly for reasons of social
publicity, rather than because of our interest to help 'bear the
burdens of others' (Gal. 6.2) in terms of a broader social concern
beyond the confines of our parochial concerns.

If we even briefly reflect on the history of our church, we will find that it has never restricted its love and philanthropy from those "outside its fold." Our contributions to the abolishment of racial segregation and on behalf of social justice, are of a most imperative nature. Our contribution to the war against ignorance, poverty, and the other physical and moral dangers which threaten the substance of our social order, are among our sacred obligations. Our resistance to the systematic effort to diminish the influence of religiously based social institutions or restrictions, such as the easing of the granting of divorces, birth control, abortion, homosexuality, free love, narcotics, pornography in print or in the theater, would undoubtedly contribute much to the improvement of the image or state of the church. Last, but by no means least, the establishment of an imperative dialogue with our children regarding the real challenges to the ethos and the confused logic of our time can no longer be delayed.[40]

Immediately following, in a section on the renewal of preaching, the Archbishop demanded that among other things, it be a "kerygma of moral integrity" and "social justice." Referring to this latter topic, he hinted at an Orthodox Christian grounding for social action.

In terms of our concern for social and moral problems, our Church is guided by the definition of our Christian obligation to man and his soul. In terms of our Church's relations toward political issues, it is guided by its centuries-old tradition that 'we cannot serve two masters' (Mt. 6.24). Its policy must be guided by its subjection to one master: God![41]

The congress topics listed were "Financial Support or Stewardship?"; "Liturgical Reform or Conscientious Religious Living?"; "Is a Fundamental Revision of our Educational Philosophy Possible?"; "Our Children: Our Pride or our Problem?"; and "What is the Future of our Church?" The latter two contain material related to social concerns. Dominant in the section on "Our Children" is clearly a deeply pained concern with the attitudes of the young people of the anti-Vietnam War period.

In the traditional Greek Orthodox family children are loved, doted over and it is in them that parents see their future, the reflection of their own dignity and find pride in the eyes of their peers. Thus, is the anguished cry, expressing the sense of betrayal and hurt felt by the parents, the result of the influence of the school?

When even students begin to speak freely—extremely freely—and demand equal rights of speech, why do they speak so disrespectfully about every authority and power, including that of their family? What is wrong? Who gave our children the right to judge our conduct? What is the dreadful thing which has changed our children from a source of pride, which we wanted them to be, to become today a challenge and a problem?

Many people ask these questions with pain and anguish some simply because they feel like expounding bitterly, others because they actually comprehend the situation, and still others as the result of sincere indignation and concern. Others see the conduct of their children as their own personal shame: others fire off barbs against the school and the church, that they have no power since they are unable to accomplish that which they have failed to accomplish themselves. Whereas others who are not parents, and who wish to present themselves as contemporary, highly educated and wise, speak of the new generation, the new art, the new civilization, without weighing the consequences of the irresponsibility, which, indeed, has no spiritual basis whatsoever.[42]

There follow several pages of sustained, if not systematic, exposition and commentary, on the situation—critical, appreciative, analytical. It deserves to be quoted extensively. Its themes are war, the relationship of parents and children, moral values, both public and private, the institutions of society, and the psychology of youth. It is a remarkable statement.

Generally speaking, opinions that are expressed and heard, are so widely divergent and so superficial, that one might well ask if it is actually true that we have the ability to think clearly any longer. The war which is being waged here in the rear echelon—the home front—will prove to be much more catastrophic than the war of shame which is being waged on the foreign front, which will have as its result the wounding of the souls, if not the actual death of the souls of millions of the youth, and we, the merchants of liberal mindedness, of intellectual anarchy, and of the prostitution of all that is sacred and holy shall be responsible. That which appears as revolution of the youth, is not as it appears: that is, the slogans, the demonstrations, violence, the raised fists, or the painted flowers and the doves. It is something much deeper and much worse: it is the revolution against every moral law—the written and the unwritten. That which makes the young rush towards revolution, is not the search to experience the freedom of conduct, black or white magic, astrology or the hypersensitive psychoses or fantasies, but the *negation of self-respect*, and *self-discipline*, which they ridicule in the most sarcastic way. This is an ideological war waged in the most covert, sophisticated and deceitful manner. The *target of this war is the moral and the intellectual integrity of the youth.* First, doubt is created in the minds of the youth regarding the religious and moral principles which they have always known. Secondly, they are made to understand that respect and love toward family and loved ones—the institution and the individuals therein—are conventional, traditional, unnatural and false. Third, they are subjected to such a merciless brainwashing, that they are rendered empty of convictions and principles, after which the void is filled with false philosophies and a frightening intellectual chaos and agony. These are the factors which bring about the insecurity, anxiety and unhappiness of our youth. As a result, they submit themselves to an ostensibly new intellectualism, which neither believes in, nor loves, nor has hope in anything. The cries against the war and in behalf of peace are most often a smoke screen, and are not actually a cause which they wish to push forward at all costs. Material affluence has given rise to a kind of pseudo-asceticism, which has nothing in common with the philosophical asceticism of Diogenes, nor with the Christian asceticism of Saint Katherine. True ascetiscism is not based simply upon the disdain or rejection of material wealth. It is based upon the exercise of those virtues which can change wealth into a means to feed the hungry and save the soul of the poor. On the other hand, the outcry against the establishment has nothing in common with the spiritual and moral activity of the revolutionaries of Alexandria, Constantinople, Jerusalem, Antioch, and Rome, who led sinful monarchs to repentance, society to moral rebirth, intellectuals to the truth of Christianity, the faithless to their spiritual redemption, the people of their times to the golden age of Christendom.

This should suffice in respect to the vociferous segment of our contemporary youth, whose reconciliation with and return to the road of common sense should be considered one of our important obligations. The youth of our day in its greater majority, however, is the same as the youth of every age. It is enthused with the ideal and welcomes it to its bosom. Under no circumstances will it condone hypocrisy. It is fanatically opposed to injustice. It angrily condemns war. It passionately loves peace. If we always realize this truth about our youth, I am certain we would be much more careful about our own conduct and the manner in which we converse with our children. When they are young, our children like to play with us and engage in pleasantries. This is also true with us. When they become older they want us to take them more seriously and find the time and have the patience to discuss their problems with them. Our children are no different than other children of the same age. The fact that they are children of parents born here or in Greece, does not make them different. Nor does the fact that they belong to the Orthodox Church automatically create within them a different manner of thinking. Quite the opposite, the consciousness of their unique dual ancestry, for which we are so proud, sharpens their criticism of us, especially when it is apparent that we are neither inspired by nor live by its principles and values. It would be good for us to take note of this fact and to see their criticism as criticism of our ethnic and religious ethos, which should make us more worthy bearers of our heritage.

Personally, I am very happy to see that we are beginning to be disturbed about our younger generation. This means that we are beginning to acquire a hopeful sensitiveness.

If it is true that the tree is judged by its fruit, and the parents by their children, and history, reality, and God condemn those unworthy generations of people as 'faithless and corrupt,' then we must also realize that now is not the time to place blame one on the other, but a 'time acceptable and a time of repentance.' Even this late hour can afford us the opportunity to call upon our conscience for the immediate fulfillment of our responsibility which we have neglected or inadequately fulfilled. [43]

The final section of the address, "What is the Future of Our Church?", began with a list of nine 'facts' regarding accomplishments; the first and last of which referred to the efforts of the Greek Orthodox Archdiocese area of social concern. [44]

In all, it was an address which not only referred to questions of social concern, but dealt at some length with one of the continuing concerns of the Church in the area of social morality: youth and its relation to family and society.

The Twenty-First Clergy-Laity Congress

The Archbishop's address at the 21st Clergy-Laity Congress held in 1972 was entitled, "A Commentary on the Congress Topics."[45]

Without any preliminaries, the commentary began a discussion of the five topics of the congress: youth, education, the parish, finance, and inter-church relations. It should be noted at once, however, that this is an "in-house" document. It focuses on the inner life of the church, and most cogently, on the parish itself rather than on the Archdiocese. The section on the parish[46] is an admirable exposition of the theology of the parish, focusing once again on its spiritual and ecclesial reality. It could well have served as the introduction to the whole.

The first section picked up on the theme of youth so predominantly emphasized in the keynote address of the 20th Clergy-Laity Congress. Its importance is highlighted in the first lines, together with the outline of the Archbishop's analysis of the causes of the crisis of youth in our day.

The first topic is that of 'our youth': a subject which is of the deepest concern to parents, priests, parish councils as well as the Archdiocese. Despite the fact that we 'all do our part,' in great measure (this we believe and say), our youth becomes more and more estranged from our accepted 'Hellenic-Christian' traditions, for the simple reason that the social environment, the American system of education, and the spiritual and cultural revolution of our times exert a far greater influence on the lives of our children in comparison with our efforts to impose our traditions as an element or structure.[47]

Analyzing the ways in which youth justifies their lack of relationship with the Church, the Primate focused on the issue of language, not so much the Greek of the liturgical services as "another language—the ecclesiastical language," the language with which the Church seeks to speak to youth of this age. The words are sharp and incisive and deserve in the context of social concern, to be recorded.

The language which the youth of today understands best is the language of hard reality or of today's struggle between traditional values and morality: and the natural and circumstantial morality which is preached in the universities, the influential newspapers and by the defenders of the great and dramatic causes of our time.

If you wish, it can be referred to as the language of confusion, a tough and vulgar language. In any case, it is the language of youth, to whom we have not tried, or are unable to teach the language of religion, the language of simplified theology, or the language of a morality, not based on instinct, but on the logic and experience of past generations, who traveled the same road of life on which the present generation finds itself. Our inability, or our unwillingness, to speak this language to our children and to reply to all their bold questions regarding their physiological life, opens wider the gap between us and our children which today is called the 'generation' or 'credibility gap,' and which, unfortunately, is a fact.[45]

A harsh critique of the parental failure to communicate spiritual values to their children followed. This, in turn, was followed by a biting critique of language spoken to the youth of our age by society at large, a critique focusing on a series of social and moral concerns. The passage concluded with a call for self-examination, re-adaptation and re-birth.

Even our society—the world in which we live—does not speak their language, according to our children. It speaks of morality, while being basically immoral. It speaks of religion, but understands it not as a spiritual exhortation, but as an institutional service at its beck and call. It speaks of education, and understands it as a means to prepare oneself for earning greater wealth. It speaks of justice and law and order and it understands it as a control of the enviroment to make it safe for society, even though it would not necessarily make it safe for those who have been wronged, or ignored or victimized. It speaks of peace, and understands it to mean that which the ancient Romans meant: a military force which would abolish the fear and danger of war, whereas the youth, who are the victims of all social, class, captitalistic, and militaristic wars, search for and demand consistency between that which is preached and that which is done. In other words, they search for another world, another society less dependent on the past, which is full of contradiction and hypocrisy, one which would permit them to be freer to adapt and orient themselves to a truly new future.

This is the problem, or chain of problems, which choke the soul of our youth, even that element of youth which has permitted itself to become involved in the fatal self-destructive activity of drug use. And our problem is simple: can we first free ourselves from our self-admiration and self-satisfaction, and become re-born in order to solve our own psychological complexes with decisiveness, and then face and solve the problems besetting our children with self-sacrifice and love? The critical nature of our times demands of us self-examination and re-adaptation of our thinking and actions. It does not permit a separation of responsibilities. Our children, who we too often consider a curse, may be a divine blessing in disguise.[49]

The final section of the commentary deals with the relationship of the Archdiocese to the ecumenical movement. It took note of criticism leveled against Orthodox involvement in ecumenism. Among the criticisms of interest to us in this study are those which come from "a number of pious and conservative laymen, who are against our relationships with the World Council of Churches and National Council of Churches, because they consider them leftist organizations, since they appear to encourage social activism, civil disorder, rebellion and communism."[50]

The Archbishop responded, but not in a direct way. He did not deny the charge. He, rather, emphasized the benefit which accrues to the Orthodox from the challenge. It is at once an answer and a call to theological study of the social and ethical issues of our times: "because of the activism or the crisis or the extreme positions taken by many churches in the World and National Council of Churches, we were better able to see the need to be vigilant and study the social, political, and moral problems of our times, to take a position in this regard, as set forth by Christ and His Bible".[51]

Twenty-Second Clergy-Laity Congress

The concluding paragraph of the keynote address to the 22nd Clergy-Laity Congress, held in Chicago in 1974 began with these words: "I am certain that you are asking: Is this the address of His Eminence?" The query is justified; this address was totally unlike any of those which had preceded it. Rather than an assessment of progress or an outline of future plans, it was a closely reasoned theological essay on the theme of the 22nd Congress, "Be ye transformed by the renewing of your mind" (Rom. 12.2).[52] A carefully reasoned exposition of the meaning of spiritual renewal for the life of the Greek Orthodox Church, is a document of permanent significance. Any attempt to summarize it will not succeed, but, in fact, will tend to distort its spirit and movement. Moreover, this address had the spirit and movement not of the enthusiastic preacher, but of the serious, calm reflection of the careful theologian as he applies the truth of the Word of God with honesty to the reality of the Church. As a theologian and professor, I recommend this document for study, not only to my colleagues and students, but also to every priest and conscientious lay person. In my judgment, it needs to be reprinted, with a new title, for general distribution.

Let it suffice to orient the reader to its major thesis. As an explication of "be ye transformed" it calls for spiritual renewal not on an emotional level, but in the sphere of thought and the orientation of our human and ecclesial wills to the will of God and the mind of Christ. This means that the church and the parish must be seen as the Body of Christ, not an organization. The theme is then applied to topics such as "The Relationship of the Faithful to the Parish" (defined by living faith and communion with God and man); "The Head of the Parish" (bishops and priests as overseers of the spiritual welfare of the flock); "The Christian and Christ" (an unbroken realtionship, permanent presence, an indestructible unity) and other such topics.

The treatment of "will" alluded to above is pertinent to ethical concerns. Throughout the talk there were references to social issues. Yet, it would take such references fully out of contest to present them as statements of social concern. They were only illustrations in the development of a very important theme for the whole life of the Church. There was, however, one passage which needs to be quoted which calls for theological study of the moral issues of our time. Let this section not only serve as evidence of the continuing and unbroken concern for social issues in this twenty-year period, but also as a sample to the reader of this notable document.

Study of Problems as a Christian Responsibility

All problems demand a logical categorization, and study according to priority. The effort toward a logical categorization we choose to call study of the problematic. However, a fair and objective study and weighing of problems can only be accomplished by an unprejudiced and enlightened mind, illuminated by the light of truth and faith. This mind St. Paul finds only in the spiritual man. And he means by this terms, the man who follows or is led by the mind of Christ. This is precisely what is sought: a mind with the degree of logical function that would not permit it to confuse the finite with the infinite, the transcendental search with tangible experience, the 'revealed truth' with epistemological research, the human intellect with the wisdom of God.

A Christian study and weighing of problems would first bring us actually face to face with moral problems. For examples, we talk of subjects or problems that refer to or affect the morality of the faithful. They are generated or caused when human behavior knowingly ignores Christian ethics for which we often hear the foolish opinion expressed, that they are so perfect they are totally unattainable in an age dominated by modern moral standards. The problems which are presented with respect to moral order, can only be solved when we recognize ethos as the strict criterion, or when we accord our conscience its role, not only of controller of our actions, but regulator as well. Therefore, moral subjects for a Christian are all that arise from disobedience to one's conscience and the correct judgment of the mind, which permit the creation of a feeling which shocks his relationship with his concience, God and his fellow man. It isn't necessary to specify the low status of these relationships, since we live their consequences: hypocrisy, insincerity, dishonesty, violence, disrespect, and their by-products—fear, destruction, crime, and corruption. Only on the wings of moral and spiritual strength does there remain a way for us to rise and be saved from our fall down the ladder of evil. For this reason our armor and weapons must be the panoply of God: truth, justice, peace, faith, supplication, vigilance, perseverance, boldness, and courage (Eph. 6.13-20), which from a subject of a sermon must become the demand and subject of our Congress. Hallucination and refutation, raving and parapsychic phenomena, contradiction and antimony, which make up the thinking of our times, could be abolished but only when the human mind is reinstated within the framework of Christian logic and undergoes a complete and radical revision and renewal. The extreme emphasis which is placed on this need is made for soley one reason: the conscientious responsibility we have definitely to put an end to extravagant thinking and speaking and false reasoning which has has become the 'logic of our times.' As a result of this 'new logic,' we have witnessed in our time these unbelievable phenomena: the justification of violence, the 'perfect' crime becomes heroic, terrorism becomes a patriotic virtue, surreptitious stealing is exalted as an achievement, betrayal of national secrets is encouraged, the subversion of accepted precepts and beliefs by people is considered service to people, character assassination remains unpunished, brainwashing becomes systematized, hedonism becomes a philsophy, pornography is justified as the abolishment of hypocrisy, and prohibition of prayer in schools is called a freedom. All the ideals of our times, such as patriotism, the family and religion all are termed outmoded and even called the reasons for the decline and moral bankruptcy of our society.

These are not the only illogical results of the new logic. According to it, practically everything that up to now has been considered illegal practices, such as abortion, homosexuality, birth control measures, pre-marital sex, prostitution, witchcraft, black magic, idolatry, discord, adultery, and practically all unlawful actions, which in pain St. Paul enumerates in his Epistle to the Christians of Galatia (Gal. 5. 19-21) must be legalized.

All these are brought to your attention with a very unconfortable feeling of inner affliction in order that you may see for yourselves how far we have been led off the track by these new concepts which influence our minds and actions, to the point that not only the accepted morality and order, but society itself and especially the life of our youth, find themselves in fatal danger.[53]

The Twenty-Third Clergy-Laity Congress

The Bicentennial observance of the United States was marked by the Greek Orthodox Archdiocese with its 23rd Clergy-Laity Congress in Philadelphia during Independence Day Week, 1976. Appropriately, the Archbishop entitled his keynote address, "The Challenge of 1976."[54] As might be expected, much of this keynote address was to focus on the meaning of the Bicentennial. Three principles—unity, liberty and trust in God—were used by the Archbishop to develop his theme. They gave him the opportunity to reiterate a strong respect for law and the view that sees most of the recent changes as harmful to society, as preludes to anarchy.

Those who would flout laws or rules or regulations always invent plausible reasons or arguments to justify the transgression, but in the last analysis they are not justified but condemned. Obedience to ecclesiastical or political statutes insures more rights than does their violation; above all it insures the right of amendment should it be required.

Whenever an attempt is made to alter the essence of a law or an established norm that has come to speak to the need and conscience of the believer or the citizen, the invariable result is to abrogate it or to supplant it with one that is osentsibly new, but which, in fact, nullifies what has stood. To provide some examples: by abolishing prayer in the schools; by removing purity from ethics; by doing legal violence against human nature itself through abortion and unnatural relations between the sexes—

far from having liberated man from prejudice and hypocrisy as some would have us believe, far from affirming his freedom and individuality, we have helped lay waste the worth of the human personality, for the preservation of which the two sacred books (the Old Testament and the New Testament) were written along with thousands of other books through the ages.[55]

It was not clear from the context what called forth this strong concern. The previously detailed encyclicals and the previously delievered keynote addresses had been strongly supportive of equality and social justice. Yet these changes, it appears also raised up a general concern for the fabric of society. Perhaps it was the tendency to interpret the changes in the laws as occasions for individualistic exploitations of liberty, thus forgetting the organic character and interrelatedness of our society. Whatever the case, the words were hard and strident.

The current attempt at a re-interpretation, or rather the arbitrary and flagrant misinterpretation of the United States Constitution or of Holy Scripture which, in its essence is a charter of morality, amounts to the total abrogation of concepts that have possessed the force of law for this nation throughout the 200 years of its existence, and for men of faith throughout the 2,000 years since the coming of Christ into the world. Already, this has led to lawlessness and anarchy as though a new law, a new charter, has been sanctioned that would re-order man's relations, not only to himself but to his fellowman, to society, and to religion. If in the third century of our nation's history, which began yesterday, this collective and individual effort persists: to tear down all legal and ethical defenses for human liberty, whether in the name of sexual equality, or greater social justice, or worse yet, man's emancipation from both moral and divine law, then we have good reason to fear that history will one day judge us as St. Paul judged the Romans saying, for although (we) knew God (we) did not honor him as God or give thanks to him, but (we) became futile in (our) thinking and (our) senseless minds were darkened. Claiming to be wise, (we) become fools. . . . (Rom. 1. 21-22).[56]

In the balance of the address, there were a few passing comments on issues of social concern, such as the family (a constantly recurring theme), but the major thrust of the address was once again spiritual and concerned with intra-church issues. However, it is significant that in the final paragraph of this Bicentennial message, the attention was turned once again to the proper addres-

sing of moral concerns by the Church. The cautious and careful
approach to the moral issues of our times was once again repeated.
It was undoubtably a word of caution to a nation which might
have allowed its proper concern for justice to have degenerated
into an uncontrolled libertarianism. Regardless, it served as evidence of a continuing concern with the social and moral issues
facing our nation on its 200th anniversary.

> Permit me at this point to observe that in matters of faith, which
> constitute the ethos and the nature and the essence of our Greek
> Orthodox way of life, we ought to be more judicious. In these
> issues of Christian faith and morals our personal interpretations
> have no place. We shall one day regret our flippancy and will
> receive a just retribution (Hebrews 2.3), to use the Apostle
> Paul's expression. And there can be no retribution more severe
> for those of us who treat lightly matters of faith and morals,
> than to see our children abandoning their spiritual and cultural
> base, losing their bearings with reference to our precious and
> historic inheritance of the spirit which is the legacy of our
> Church and of our people. To echo one more admonition of
> Paul, counting it a sacred obligation to ourselves but also
> to the generations that will succeed us, Only let us hold true
> to what we have attained, and be of one mind (Phil.3.16).[57]

The Twenty-Fourth Clergy-Laity Congress

The commitment of the Greek Orthodox Archdiocese, in the
person of Archbishop Iakovos, to addressing and dealing with
issues of social concern came to a high point in the keynote address to the 24th Clergy-Laity Congress of 1978 in Detroit, Michigan.[58]

The theme of the Congress was "Be ye doers of the Word and
and not hearers only" (James 1.22). This most promising text for
dealing with issues of Christian social ethics was not to remain
unfulfilled despite the fact that, as the Archbishop announced,
this 24th Congress was "not a mere continuation of past congresses.
It is a Charter Congress."[59] The Detroit Congress adopted a new
charter for the Archdiocese which established a synod of bishops,
decentralizing much of the authority of the Church. One is not
surprised to note that much of the address referred to the restructuring of the Archdiocese and its meaning. For the Archbishop,
this new direction focused much more responsibility upon the
local church, understood both as diocese and the parishes which

constitute it. Familiar themes are used to evoke the proper meaning of this new direction: unity (parish-diocese-archdiocese), spiritual life (unity with Christ), ecumenical vision as true Orthodoxy (as opposed to mere conservatism or 'Orthodox puritanism'), and finally struggle for growth and transformation of personal, church, and public life.

It is all the more remarkable that with the focus on the restructuring of the administrative life of the Archdiocese, this address came back again and again to broadly and narrowly conceived issues of social concern.

Thus, an early definition of the mission of the restructured church is presented in the context of the Kingdom of God in this nation. "The mission assigned to us by the Provident Father in Heaven, therefore, is to humbly labor together with all American believers, so that His Kingdom, a kingdom of love and justice may come, and that His Will, aimed at substituting error with truth and perdition with salvation, may be done on earth by all, as it is in heaven."[60] Among the benefits of the restructuring which Archbishop Iakovos foresaw were several opportunities for personal and corporate growth by the Greek Orthodox faithful. He concluded his list of benefits to come from the restructuring with this expecttation, indicating a concern for the social mission of the Church.

> It enables us to cope with situations on a local level. . . and develop vital new patterns and norms so essential for a direct confrontation with problems of a moral and ethical nature. This would contribute, as nothing else would, to the growth and expansion of the Orthodox Faith and Tradition.[61]

In a subsequent section, he underlined the problems which the restructuring presented to the congress for solution. This afforded the opportunity to the forward-looking hierarch to launch into an involved expression of concern for the contact of the Church with the "intellectual, moral and social problems which surround us." This statement was of significance for the relation it occupied to the whole of the address. The original transcript covered slightly more than twenty-seven pages. The statement below was included in three full pages. When one considers the context, the focus on the inner reorganization of the structure of the Archdiocese, three full pages bore solid witness to the depth of conviction of the Archbishop to the issues of social concern. Though critical, even condemnatory, the Archbishop encouraged his church to come to grips with the perspective. Moreover, he concluded with hope, believing that the truth of the faith, when correctly applied to the social problems of our times, can find and implement the solutions. In this writer's opinion, care and attention are due this passage as the Church enters the decade of the eighties.

Another problem which I am afraid will be with us for a long time is whether or not we can cope with our ever-changing society which, under the influence of new scientific findings and the impact of the so-called situational ethics and 'new morality' puts to test the values and principles which we profess to believe. Are we to yield and abandon them thereby accepting the new situation, or are we fortified with such knowledge and experience so as to resist and fight? To be more clear and precise, I refer to the intellectual, moral and social problems which surround us, pressing our minds and our hearts for answers, while forcing us to judge for ourselves whether or not we are truly victims of antedated, anachronistic and obsolete beliefs, or the defenders of the changeless values of Christianity against attempts by modern quasi-ethics to unseat spirituality and moral sensitivity from the place they have occupied for centuries as the molders of our ethos and the fashioners of human behavior.

The problems of today, as we all know, range from the materialistic and technological or physiological concept of life, to its mystical and extrasensory perception, from a theory which would reduce or eliminate childbirth through the legalization of contraceptives and abortion—born from a concern for mankind as a result of the population explosion—to a noble and lofty interest in ecology which concerns itself with the preservation of even the lowest form of animal and vegetable life; from the equal rights amendment, to sexual and child abuse; from the beautiful goals of UNICEF and Youth Year, to child prostitution; from scientific research to prolong human life, to street and park and subway crime; from an effort to modernize and perfect education, to the license to protect the rights of those who have made obscenity and pornography a lucrative industry; from an effort to strengthen the arm of the judiciary, to its abolishment as cruel and inhuman; from the declaration that all men are created equal and free, to the defense of those who have no regard for human rights and dignity or freedom; finally, from the belief that violators of the law should be censured, impeached and severely punished, to the practice of clemency which returns evil-doers to society, particularly the rapists, the burglars, the drug peddlers and the killers.

The problem of how to meet and resolve these problems—which are problems of inconsistency, contradiction, and antinomy between words and deeds and between conscience and actual behavior—will have to stay with us until the day when American Christians wake up, realize their impotence and find their way back to the never-exhausted spring-well of and ever-new and refreshing spiritual power, i.e. God and His Will and Word, as it is recorded in the Bible and in the annals of Christian, Greek and American history and experience. Those who claim that the clock cannot be turned back would do well to take a good, long hard look at the appearance of modern men and women and to their situational ethics, as attested to by their moral license, their lust, their greed, and their lack of respect for human life, property, honor and welfare. Because of the history of their Church, Orthodox believers should not allow themselves self-acquittal and by the same token condemn someone else, whether it be society or those at the service of mankind; i.e., educators, clergy, politicians or civic leaders. A similar reaction to the problems would indict us as doers of a double injustice, both to ourselves as well as to others. For God has endowed all and deprived none, of logic, judgement and the ability to self-examine and self-control. Furthermore, God gave to His people a Charter, the value of which cannot be challenged, i.e. the Bible—that book of human aspiration and inspiration and prophets and apostles and martyrs and confessors—from whom to choose their example for emulation and perfection.

Orthodox believers who find themselves confronted with such perplexing and unresolved problems, should exercise more prudence and show greater maturity. If instead of groaning and moaning for the alleged indifference that God, Church and Society display, they should choose to search and find within their minds and souls the ability to better understand these problems.

For I believe and together with you, that the compassionate understanding and the proper approach of a problem leads, as nothing else does, to its solution, Such an approach, besides helping a given problematic situation, would uplift our soul and spirit and change our agony into ecstasy, and our worries into true rejoicing. [62]

The issue, however, of concern for social problems was not dropped as the talk proceeded. In the area of inter-Orthodox cooperation, the Archbishop called for joint study committees to deal with a variety of problems, including the "moral problems common to all."[63] But he did not restrict this concern to study: ". . .we must also concern ourselves with our Orthodox brothers throughout the World, and do all we can to assist them in their fight against inhumanity, oppression and persecution."[64] There were additional references to social concern in the keynote address. One was a positive statement on the meaning of commitment to country. This definition, in the spirit of the motto of the conference included the conviction that we are "to do everything that would contribute to its spiritual, moral, political and social welfare."[65]

The epilogue of this address made an appeal for world peace and for the strengthening of American family life. It also included a call to three commitments: commitment to increased Christian social action wherever and whenever the trumpet calls, be it Constantinople, Greece, Cyprus, Lebanon, Israel, the Arab countries, Rhodesia, South Africa or Eastern Europe; commitment to protest unwise or harmful use of authority and commitment to protect those who suffer because of it, rallying all our moral and spiritual forces in defense of their rights.[66]

Thus, ten clergy-laity congresses provide a substantial amount of evidence for an ongoing tradition of concern for social issues. Hardly a keynote address has been without reference to social concerns. A careful student will note affirmations and concern which remain unchanged. It is possible as well to perceive changed emphases, even levels of confidence and hope. But what the evidence abundantly supports is the conclusion that social concerns have had a permanent place in the keynote addresses of Archbishop Iakovos to the clergy-laity congresses of his church.

NOTES

The intent of this article is to present archival and other material not readily available in English for the study of the moral and social concerns of the Greek Orthodox Archdiocese of North and South America. Consequently, extensive quotations are used not only for illustrative purposes, but primarily as resource material for use by students of ethics and those concerned with the history of Eastern Orthodox Christianity in the Americas.

1. See Exetastes, *Contemporary Issues* (New York, 1976).

2. Archives, Mimeographed typescript translated from the Greek text, pp. 16-18.

3. Ibid., p. 18.

4. Archives, Mimeographed typescript. "The Message of Archbishop Iakovos. Before the First General Assembly of the Sixteenth Congress of the Greek Orthodox Archdiocese of North and South America. Boston, MA., June 25, 1962," pp. 1-2.

5. Ibid., pp. 6-11.

6. Ibid., p. 7.

7. Ibid., p. 3.

8. Ibid., p. 35.

9. Ibid., p. 37.

10. Archives, "Prelude," mimeographed text.

11. Ibid., p. 2.

12. Ibid., pp. 3, 4.

13. Ibid., p. 5.

14. Ibid.

15. Ibid., p. 11.

16. Ibid., p. 40.

17. Archives, "Archbishop's Address to the Eighteenth Biennial Clergy-Laity Congress of North and South America. Montreal; June 27, 1966."

18. Ibid., p. 1.

19. Ibid., p. 2.

20. Ibid., p. 3.

21. Ibid., p. 7.

22. Ibid., p. 8.

23. Ibid.

24. Ibid., pp. 8-9.

25. Ibid., p. 9.

26. Ibid., pp. 9-10.

27. *Proceedings of the Nineteenth Clergy-Laity Congress of the Communities of the Greek Orthodox Archdiocese of North and South America, Athens, July 20-21, 1968.*

28. Ibid., pp. 34-44.

29. Ibid., p. 34.

30. Ibid., pp. 35-36.

31. Ibid., pp. 43-44.

32. Ibid., p. 36.

33. Ibid., p. 38.

34. Ibid., p. 37.

35. Ibid., p. 41.

36. Ibid., p. 44.

37. Ibid., p. 43.

38. Ibid., p. 40.

39. *Towards the Decade 1970-1980: Keynote Address by His Eminence Archbishop Iakovos to the Delegates of the 20th Biennial Clergy-Laity Congress of the Greek Orthodox Archdiocese of North and South America, June 29, 1970.* Offset typescript text.

40. Ibid., pp. 4-5.

41. Ibid., p. 5.

42. Ibid., p. 16.

43. Ibid., pp. 16-19.

44. Ibid., pp. 20-21.

45. *The Greek Orthodox Archdiocese of North and South America. 21st Biennial Clergy-Laity Congress. July 1-8, 1972. Rice Hotel, Houston, Texas. A commentary on the Congress Topics, by Archbishop Iakovos.* Offset typescript text.

46. Ibid., pp. 30-34.

47. Ibid., p. 25. The Greek text precedes the English text.

48. Ibid., pp. 26-27.

49. Ibid., pp. 27-28.

50. Ibid., pp. 39-40.

51. Ibid., p. 40.

52. *Decisions of the 22nd Clergy-Laity Congress of the Greek Orthodox Archdiocese of North and South America in Chicago, Illinois, June 30-July 7, 1974.* pp. 116-25.

53. Ibid., pp. 122-23. It should be noted that in addition to the keynote address another address was also delivered by Archbishop Iakovos entitled "Along the Shores of Our Concerns" which treated with many of the usual keynote address topics. Ibid., pp. 110-15. Here, Watergate and the need for "purifying the much polluted atmosphere of the nation" (p. 111). There is a new familiar litany of the moral ills of the times (p. 112); an extensive treatment of the sanctity of the body (p. 113) and appeals for actions (pp. 114-115).

54. *Decisions of the 23rd Clergy-Laity Congress of the Greek Orthodox Archdiocese of North and South America in Philadelphia, PA., July 2-9, 1976.* p. 123.

55. Ibid.

56. Ibid., p. 125.

57. Ibid., p. 131.

58. *Keynote Address delivered by His Eminence Archbishop Iakovos, 24th Biennial Congress, July 1-8, 1978, Detroit, MI.* Offset text.

59. Ibid., p. 4.

60. Ibid., pp. 12-13.

61. Ibid., pp. 15-18.

62. Ibid., p. 20.

63. Ibid.

64. Ibid., p. 24.

65. Ibid., p. 26.

Chapter Four

SOCIAL CONCERN AND THE
SOCIAL AND MORAL ISSUES COMMITTEES

The Biennial Clergy-Laity Congresses of the Greek Orthodox
Archdiocese are much more than a legislative agency of the Church.
They are a forum where the leadership of the Church gathers,
both clergy and laity, to accomplish other kinds of goals as well.
It might, on the other hand, be thought of as some kind of vast
sacramental, which manifests and expresses the inner reality —
with all its tensions and unresolved perplexities — of a living and
vibrant Church, yet which declares for all to see an essential
divinely given unity of God's people. It is, as we have seen in the
previous chapter, a place where the hierarchical leadership of the
Church seeks to provide long-term direction and guidance, nudging
the hearts and minds of the local parish leadership in the directions
the Church as a whole is to move. Understood this way, the Clergy-
Laity Congress is an exercise in Christian nurturance.

On the other hand, the Clergy-Laity Congresses are a place where
the people of God present their own concerns and interests to the
hierarchy and lay-leadership of the Archdiocese, sensitizing it to
the strong undercurrents flowing through the ecclesial *soma*. As
such it has the characteristic of the ancient Greek *Agora* where
ideas and views were exchanged, alliances formed and interest
groups mobilized. It is this and more. In this study we wish to
reflect upon one other side of these Congresses—their place as an
expression of Orthodox Christian social conscience.

In the first instance some background on the Clergy-Laity Congresses themselves, and the manner of their committee organization needs to be discussed. This so that the question of the significance and authority of the pronouncements on social and moral issues may be evaluated. Secondly, an overview of the decisions
adopted by the Clergy-Laity Congresses with particular reference
to the work of the Social and Moral Issues Committees will be
presented. A cross reference to the social ethics topics discussed
and approved by the Congresses will conclude this chapter.

The Nature of the Social and Moral Issues Committee Decisions

In many cases, the Clergy-Laity Congresses have been the locus and the occasions at which the long-term concerns of the hierarchical leadership of the Church found a certain resonance and response on the part of the clergy and laity, permitting and encouraging its concrete manifestation. It would seem that this is the pattern which best describes the history of the Social and Moral Issues Committees during the 60's and 70's. As we have seen, from the very beginning of his hierarchical service as Archbishop of the Greek Orthodox Church in the Americas, Archbishop Iakovos offered a new vision to a Church which had traditionally kept aloof from the social concerns of the larger society. Since those first modest and simple expressions signifying a return to the ancient and Byzantine traditions of social concern and involvement, a remarkable change has taken place in the conception of the work of a Clergy-Laity Congress. Previous to 1960, the year of the first Clergy-Laity Congress over which Archbishop Iakovos presided, not a hint of social concern for the larger society can be discerned in the recorded acts and decisions; that year marked a change which has made it impossible to concerive of a Clergy-Laity Congress today which would not speak to the social issues of the day.

It is true that the desire for this kind of Orthodox Christian social witness had been expressed as early as 1956 at the 13th Clergy-Laity Congress. But it fell on deaf ears. It was only when the Archbishop, at the conclusion of the 15th Clergy-Laity Congress (his first) in Buffalo, New York, in 1960 – concluded the sessions with a "Message to the Press" did the outlines of the future movement of the Church on these issues emerge. The message was "an official statement on aims and purposes."[1] The first of its seven points was a revolutionary change in orientation. It referred to the Greek Orthodox Church's "Mission which is to exert to its fullest extent its spiritual, cultural, and moral influence in America. The members of the Church are committed to combat all phases of current social evil prevalent today." The list of examples that follows sounds a bit quaint to the sophisticated ear two decades later. But the important thing is the turn toward the social environment; the outward look which saw the society in which the Greek Orthodox Church found itself, not simply as the alien "them," but as a field of concern, a context for the Church's life which could no longer be ignored, but which had to be addressed. Understood this way, this reorientation of perspective of the Clergy-Laity Congresses was one of the most important signs that a Church which was until then an immigrant community isolated from the larger society, was beginning to reach out in responsible Christian conscience to the larger society—a part of which it increasingly felt itself to be.[2]

As such, it was a genuine expression of Christian outreach and an embodiment of the sense of Christian mission. The "Message to the Press" of 1960 not only made reference to the moral order and the strengthening of spiritual values in the society at large, but also raised issues of peace in the world, justice, service to the nation and to humanity, as well as ecumenical concerns. It proved to be something more than a mere press release. It was a charter document for the expression of social concerns by the Church.

Beginning with the 17th Clergy-Laity Congress in Denver, Colorado (1964), a history of outspoken stands on numerous issues of social concern begins to unfold. It seems that the 16th Clergy-Laity Congress was devoted to matters of internal organization, a not unexpected step for the new Archbishop. However, it was not until the 18th Clergy-Laity Congress in 1966 that a Committee on Social Concerns was included in the organizational format of the Congress. Since then, every Clergy-Laity Congress has included not only a Committee on Social Concerns, but also in separate resolutions and in other committees, there have been frequent additional expressions of social concern.

The structure of the Social Concerns Committee is the same as that of all Clergy-Laity Committees. Prior to the Congress the organizing committee announces which committees will function and the names of the leaders of the committees. Earlier, Social and Moral Issues Committees had a chairman and a rapporteur forming the committee leadership. Thus, for example, the 20th Clergy-Laity Congress Social and Moral Issues Committee (1970) had a priest as chairman, Rev. Constantine Volaitis, and a layman, Judge Christ Seraphim as rapporteur. The next Congress, however, saw a system established which hence has become standard procedure. A bishop is appointed convener of the committee and a chairman or co-chairmen are appointed to actually conduct the meetings. Thus, in 1972 in Houston, Texas, Bishop Meletios of Christianoupolis was the Social and Moral Issues Committee Convener, and Mayor George A. Athanson and Rev. Dr. Stanley S. Harakas were co-chairmen of the Committee. The involvement of the bishop varies according to the interest of the individual hierarch. Bishop Meletios, for example, was deeply committed to the work of the Committee, and was eager to promote his own strongly conservative views quite vigorously. Other bishops merely exercised oversight on the work of the Committee. It is perhaps a sign of the times that one of the recent Clergy-Laity Congresses in 1980, held in Atlanta, Georgia, had a woman as its Social and Moral Issues Committee Chairperson, Attorney Elenie Huszagh.

The commitee members have usually chosen to serve on the basis of their own interest. In recent years a pre-congress indication of preference has led to prepared committee lists, but these are not rigidly enforced. Thus, persons making up the Committee are there because of interest.

In addition, resource persons of special expertise are frequently asigned to the committee.

The committee forms its own agenda, discusses the issues, and prepares a report which is then submitted to the General Assembly of the Congress where it is proposed for adoption, discussed, modified, and voted upon, topic by topic. It is subject to the usual parliamentary maneuvers and occasionally has been the victim of controversial rulings by the chair. Discussion and modification of the report from the floor is not an unusual occurrence.

It is important to understand this ordering of the committee so as to see the reports in the correct light. Each report stands on its own and reflects the concrete concerns and views of those who prepared it. Thus it is possible to discern differing emphases, terminology, approaches and, in some issues, even varying ethical stances. Yet, by and large, they form a coherent body of teaching and moral pronouncement.

The question arises as to their authority. In what sense can these pronouncements be considered "official?" The Clergy-Laity Congresses themselves exist in some sort of "canonical cloud." As originally conceived and implemented, the Clergy-Laity Congresses had as their sphere of action and concern the financial and organizational life of the parishes. Doctrinal matters are specifically excluded from the concerns of the Clergy-Laity Congresses. As a legislative forum and body, the authority is given to the Clergy-Laity Congresses to decide on matters of financial support for the national programs (the Finance Committee always has the largest membership) and constitutional structure. Traditionally, it has also been a sounding board in which local views on such disparate concerns as Relgious Education, Youth and Young Adult Programming, Camping, Greek Language and Cultural Education, Philanthropy, Publications, Collegiate and Theological Education, Missions, etc. have been expressed. While the biennial budgets for these programs are approved by the congresses and receive reports on each of these actitivities, the major oversight and policy direction has come not from the Clergy-Laity Congresses but from the Archdiocesan Council, which is appointed by and responsible to the Archbishop. In 1978 the Archdiocese set aside its system of Archdiocesan districts in which all bishops were suffragans and returned to the more ecclesially correct synodical system, in which the bishops are ruling ecclesial authorities over specific ecclesial territories. Traditionally, it is neither a Clergy-Laity Congress, nor an Archdiocesan Council which pronounces on issues of moral concern, but a synod of bishops. It is for this reason that on matters of moral and social concern particularly, a measure of confusion exists as to the authority, significance and status of the Social and Moral Issues Committee decisions of the Clergy-Laity Congresses.

A key to the answer to this question is found in the practice which has existed since the founding of the Clergy-Laity system requiring the submission of the decisions of the Congresses to the Ecumenical Patriarchate of Constantinople for ratification. By and large with only very few exceptions, the Patiarchate routinely approves the decisions of the Congress.

Yet by no stretch of the imagination would the Patriarchate think of itself as bound or limited to decisions on moral questions by the Congress' statements. It is clear that, except for concretely administrative actions for local application, the other pronouncements and actions are expressive of an Orthodox consciousness and serve as an indicator of the general position of the Greek Orthodox Church in the Americas, but not much more than that. Given the kind of ecclesiology which is characteristic of Orthodoxy in general, which accords a concrete authority to the bishops and a more amorphous — yet quite real authority — to the spiritual, moral and doctrinal consciousness of the Body of Christ, it seems clear that the judgments expressed by the Moral and Social Issues Committee reports, as adopted by the Clergy-Laity Congresses, represent in a fairly clear way the 'mind of the Church' in these matters. Yet in no way may they be considered binding in an absolute sense. This is especially true, it would seem, as it refers to the rationale presented for each of the positions espoused. In the western milieu in which we find ourselves the 'official' Orthodox position on controversial issues is often requested. For the Orthodox, there is no hesitancy in the articulation of concrete and specific views on many issues, but the designation of these views as 'official' is problematic. Only the decisions of an Ecumenical Synod on an issue of doctrinal importance could be described as official in the fullest sense. Practically speaking, however, the closest we could come to an official position would be one which was adopted by most or all of the Orthodox Churches in the world at some pan-Orthodox meeting. Lacking that, the next best expression of the formal views of Orthodoxy on a subject would be a concurrence of expressed views by the holy synods of autocephalous and autonomous Orthodox Churches throughout the world. Thus, the decisions of the Clergy-Laity Congresses on social and moral issues can be seen only as expressions of the mind of the Church in this place, which on the one hand serve as platforms for influencing the society in which the Church finds itself and as an exercise in spiritual nurture of the membership of the Church itself. As such, they will also serve to inform the synod of bishops under the chairmanship of the local church's primate regarding such matters. A synodal decision, then, whether based on these reports or not, would be the vehicle for expressing (in a measure) the official views of an Orthodox Church in this place and this time. In this sense, such a position would express the official view of the Greek Orthodox Archdiocese of North and South America, a view, it must be noted, which could be superseded by a larger synodal decision—whether it be patriarchal, pan-Orthodox, or ecumenical.

In conclusion, there is some question about the approach to these documents which seeks in them an official view. If pressed, the answer would have to be that they are not official. In a procedural sense, they may be considered as a step in the process by which the local synod of bishops might choose to speak on these topics. From a pastoral perspective these reports of the Social and Moral Issues Committees of the Clergy-Laity Congresses serve in several important ways. They at once are an outreach of the Church into the larger society; they seek to protect the body of the faithful from wrong opinion; they also are a means for forming and educating the members of the Church. Yet, at the same time—and probably most important — they are the expression of the consciousness of the Church on these issues of moral and social concern. As such, they have an authority which transcends the juridical concept of officiality, reflecting rather the spiritual, doctrinal and ethical mind of the Church.

Thus, to quote a decision of the Clergy-Laity Congress on a social and moral issue does not provide a fully official response to the question addressed. But not to see it as a manifestation of the living core of the Greek Orthodox Church's conscience would be overlooking its deeper, perhaps more abiding significance. Thus, there is a sense in which these pronouncements are in no way absolute or final. But in another sense, they have a definitive character to them—they *are* an unmistakable and concrete expression of the spiritual values and moral norms of the Greek Orthodox Archdiocese in the Americas. Until something more official is produced, these reports will continue to serve as a primary witness to the social conscience of Greek Orthodoxy in the western hemisphere.

A Chronicle of Concerns

As was noted above, the purpose of this work is not to analyze the texts, but only to present them for further study. Chapter Five of this volume presents the texts of the Clergy-Laity Congresses for the period under discussion. Here, we wish to present an overview and a brief synopsis of the teaching contained in them.

In what might be called the pre-history of the Social and Moral Issues Committees, it is interesting to note that the first major concern of a genuinely disinterested character was regarding civil rights. The Archbishop, as Chairman of the Standing Conference of Canonical Orthodox Bishops, an extra-canonical body of inter-jurisdictional cooperation, had encouraged the promulgation in April of 1964, a strong statement supporting the black cause. The 17th Clergy-Laity Congress held three months later, endorsed the the SCOBA declaration.[3]

Montreal, Canada, was the site of the 18th Clergy-Laity Congress in 1966 which had the first duly constituted Social and Moral Issues Committee. It entered into its task with vigor and enthusiasm, producing a report of wide-ranging concern.[4] Brief statements were issued on the following seven topics: Human Rights, World Peace, Moral Disintegration in the Nation, Crime and Juvenile Delinquency, Alcoholism and Narcotics, the Underprivileged, and Social Action. There is no mention of the names of the Committee leadership in the official record of the decisions of this Congress. This Congress also touched on other issues of social and moral concerns in the work of two other Committees. The Committee on the Church and Spiritual Issues addressed briefly the issue of secularism. It described "the dichotomy of religion and culture" perceived as growing in the American mileau as "alien to Orthodoxy" and as a phenomenon which was creating "increasing spiritual problems." Further, the auspicious beginning of Greek Orthodox Archdiocese expression on issues of public concern was also embodied in the existence and report of the Committee on Church and Family. This report decried the "moral and spiritual crisis" in the family, analyzing its causes into its moral, spiritual, cultural and sociological roots. The report called the clergy and the laity to face the "unprecedented responsibility," "to save the family from further deterioration," and described the only sure cure to the malaise of the family today as a "mission...to guide the family toward Christ."

Athens, Greece, was the site of the 19th Clergy-Laity Congress, held from July 20 to 27, 1968.[5] The report of the Moral and Social Issues Committee addressed a number of new issues, which, in spite of the locale of the congress, were treated exclusively in the context of the North American cultural and social reality. Approved as read by the General Assembly, the report came to grips with several issues which had received little or no attention in the past by Orthodox theologians. The topics covered were: secularism and the relations of the Church to it; Christian reaction to the influence of the mass media; the dignity of man; the question of civil disobedience with special reference to the draft and the law; crime, war and peace. Thus, the congress held on the question of secularism that it was not only "the greatest challenge to the Christian Church," but it was described as "the underlying cause of every social and political ill of modern man." As a consequence this section of the report pronounced that "the greatest single task facing the Christian world today is to make the great central truths of the Christian faith relevant to today's man." It called for a translation of these truths to the "idiom of modern man" and for an "experimental center" for the study and realization of these goals.

The section on the mass media assessed the contemporary importance and impact of the media, focusing much attention on the extreme power of "a handful of media makers" and decrying "the violence and indecent and obscene elements flowing into our homes and society." It proceeded, however, to call for more effective use of the media by the Church. The short statement on the diginity of man delineated certain human rights, including freedom from "the degrading and soul-killing qualities of hopeless poverty." The fourth topic addressed was "Civil Disobedience—The Draft and the Law." While recognizing the right to "organized and lawful demonstration" the report opposed the use of violence and irresponsible acts. It opposed the burning of draft cards with an appeal to the necessity to preserve freedom "when those sacred rights are threatened." This was a topic which was to be subject to significant revision as the years went by.

The increase of crime in our society was deplored and was responded to by asking for "strict law enforcement" by police and the courts, calling for "social self-protection" and the "reasserting of authority where authority belongs." There was no reference to the social causes of crime. It should be noted that the Chairman of the 1968 Committee, Chris Seraphim, was a criminal court Judge. The final section on "War and Peace" roundly condemned the evil of war but also decried the "alternatives (which) are sometimes a nightmare beyond comprehension." The section ends with an appeal that the powers involved in the Vietnam War "take seriously the pursuit of peace." In addition to the Social and Moral Issues Report, there was also a report on immigration questions faced by the Church regarding new arrivals from Greece to the United States with concern for their integration into the life of the Greek-American religious community; certainly a most interesting sociological indication of the changes having taken place over the decades. Immigrants were no longer'us'; they were 'them.'

1970 brought the Clergy-Laity to New York City, the location of the Archdiocesan headquarters. The report of the Social and Moral Issues Committee[6] began—significantly, for this study—with the judgment that, "It is no longer necessary to argue for the need of our Church to speak clealy and act consistently in areas of moral and social concern." This led to a renewal of a request, which had been often repeated, for the establishment of an office of social concerns. The job description was thorough. Its task

would be to inform priests and parishes of the Orthodox Church's positions on current issues, set priorities, help Parishes and Archdiocesan Districts respond in meaningful ways to the issues of the day in their local areas, assist the parishes to organize local social action committees and provide direction and guidance for them to function, and finally, inform and inspire general action through frequent communication, with a newsletter.

Eventually, with an Office of Social Concern on the Archdiocesan level, programs and action on the Archdiocesan District level and in state, regional and local areas could be implemented.

The report also called for the formulation of position papers on numerous topics of moral and social concern, a suggestion which would become more and more an approach to be followed by subsequent committees.

Some new issues were included in the report of the 1970 Con-

gress. Drug abuse, abortion, pornography, and ecology were discussed for the first time, while the topics of race relations, war and
peace and crime and lawlessness were again addressed by the committee.

The report on Drug Abuse called for the retention and strengthening of existing laws, especially those which outlawed the use of
marijuana. The report briefly mentions, in addition, the causes of
drug addiction, the need for adequate instruction of youth regarding
drug abuse, the rehabilitation of those involved in drugs and the
provision of "an environment of Christian love and faith" as one
solution to the problem.

The Committee decried the recently passed New York abortion
law. A sense of urgency and alarm pervades this portion of the
report. The traditional Orthodox opposition to abortion infused
an unusually strong—and again, from the point of view of this
study, signficant—statement which also for the first time in these
documents, referred to the Church's role in society as "prophetic."
The report said, "We first must give a clarion call to all the people
of our nation, warning them of this serious violation of the reverence of life by the indiscriminate exercise of abortion. It is our
prophetic responsibility to condemn this law as immoral." The
second part of the report on abortion directed its attention to
pastoral guidance for the members of the Church on this issue.

Both the issues of pornography and ecology were addressed in
short paragraphs, the first deploring the spread of pornography
and calling for its elimination; and the second, expressing gratitude
to the nation's young people for raising ecological concerns to
public attention and calling upon the "citizens of this land and of
the whole world. . . to reduce to the absolute minimum the defilement of our enviroment. . ."

Among the previously dealt with topics, the section on race
relations was the longest and the most carefully developed. Of
interest to this study was the conscious reference to the Archbishop's statement on racism in the Congress' Keynote Address
which was quoted verbatim in the Report of the Committee.
The report was wide-ranging in its analysis and made reference
not only to the racial injustices perpetrated against blacks, but
also to Mexican-American migrant workers and the poverty-
struck condition of American Indians. Four specific suggestions
were recommended to the Church for social action, couched in
the language of Christian values. The report on War and Peace
repeated its approval "of every effort and every movement to term-

inate war and hostility in every area." There was no reference, however, to the previously articulated defense of freedom or the criticism of the draft card burnings. It was clearly reflective of the change in the nation's perception of the war in Vietnam. The report on crime and lawlessness, however, showed little; there was a demand "that our people receive adequate protection"; that "public order is in jeopardy," and the judgment that if public order "breaks down, freedom will be lost." Again "peaceful assembly" was encouraged and respected. No reference to violent civil disobedience was made. Chairman of the committee was Rev. Constantine Volaitis and rapporteur was Judge Chris Seraphim.

The most thorough extensive and organized report of the Moral and Social Issues Committee was prepared and adopted at the 21st Clergy-Laity Congress in Houston, Texas, in 1972.[7] Divided into three sections, the report was remarkably comprehensive. Among the new topics discussed was the whole first section, entitled, "Measures for the Development of an Orthodox Christian Social Conscience." Included were the following striking statements: "There is need to raise the consciousness of our people regarding the implications of our Orthodox Christian faith to the social issues of our time." The committee felt that the time had come "for Orthodox Christians of America to challenge themselves and the people of our nation with the affirmation that Christ is Lord of all the world and that He is the answer to the problems of every society."

The second part of the 21st Congress Social and Moral Issues Report addressed "Social and Moral questions in the Parish Life" with a completely new, and sustained treatment which includes the topics: the Church as the 'leaven' of society; the integrity of the church's message and parish practice; making decisions for parish life; the task of our parishes in the coming years; individual employment and our identity as Orthodox Christians; and finally, organizing for effective diakonia. The Congress called for diocesan and local parish social and moral issues committees in this last segment. It is clear that the movement begun years before by the Archbishop in terms of moral and social outreach, and which had become firmly established on the clergy-laity level now, had begun what has proven to be a difficult to implement, yet unmistakable tendency for the embodiment of social and moral issues in the spheres of the diocese and the parish. Subsequent congresses continue to press for the practical and local application of what, by and large until this Congress, were pronouncements from on high.

The third part of this report entitled, "Facing the Social Issues of the World" addressed several topics which had previously been spoken to by earlier Congresses: drug abuse, race relations, law and order with justice, and peace. A new topic, introduced in its own right but which had been touched upon in the treatment of various other topics in the past, was "the family in contemporary society." The committee held that "the family's declining influence is a major factor behind much of our society's current disorientation." The committee placed under this rubric a number of current trends which contributed to the family's breakdown.

> With this in mind, the Social and Moral Issues Committee views with great alarm current trends of social and moral deterioration which are contrary to Christian ethics and practice. Among the more disturbing elements of this trend are: the breakdown of traditional family relationsips; the confusion over the social and moral roles of male and female; the increase in crime and acts of violence; the strong pressure for abortions, and the increasing prevalence in the mass media of pornographic and other salacious materials which seek to exploit man's weaknesses rather than elevate his sights to new spiritual and philanthropic levels.

Within this report on the family were also some first tentative statements on homosexuality, venereal disease and sexual promiscuity. Also, some lines were directed to the role of mothers as "co-creators," and the need to understand non-Christian ideologies such as "witchcraft, astrology, occult forms, and other so-called exotic religions which promote superstition and anti-Christian attitudes."

Among the previously treated issues, the section on "Law and Order with Justice" provided significant balance to the previous two congress reports on the subject, while reiterating pleas for the protection of the public through "vigorous law and order support on all levels of government." This report, however, included a call for "constructive court reform procedures," for "prison reform," and for an integration of "freedom, order and justice."

The section on 'peace' was a most explicit repetition of the call for peace in Vietnam through the efforts of national leaders. The reference to war was an exlusively negative critique. There was also an appeal to the consciences of the faithful to work for peace. The passage is poignant:

> We who have been called the "sons of God" when we pursue the avenues that make peace, pledge ourselves to labor in all possible ways to bring peace in Vietnam. No time can be too

soon for the conclusion of this tragic war.

Convener of the committee was Bishop Meletios of Christianoupolis; and co-chairmen were the mayor of Hartford, Connecticut, George A. Athanson and Professor Stanley S. Harakas.

The extent of the Houston report on social and moral issues seemed, two years later in 1974, to cause a reflective attitude in the Committee on Social and Moral Issues at the 22nd Clergy-Laity Congress in Chicago, Illinois.[8]

The Committee gave itself the assignment "to review the accomplishments of the past and to define the task of the Greek Orthodox Archdiocese for the ensuing two years in this area." Concern about the Office of Social and Moral Issues was again expressed, as was the raising of "the consciousness of our people regarding the implications of our Orthodox Christian Faith for the social issues of our time." And again, the implications of the Church's social and moral teaching for parish life was emphasized. All this was included in the lead section entitled: "Measures for the Development of an Orthodox Christian Social Conscience." For the first time, portions of the previous Committee's report were repeated verbatim in the subsequent Committee's report. The second section of the Chicago report repeated the Houston paragraph on the "Church as the leaven of society." It also readdressed the topic: "The Orthodox Christian faith versus certain fundraising methods," while repeating both the critical mood and moral substance of the former report, but with changed wording. It also proposed a resolution which stated that "this Congress reaffirms the teachings of the Church on abortion..."

All of this seemed to be addressing the very real problem of consciousness raising concerning social issues on the local level. Even the abortion resolution primarily directed itself not to society at large, but to the Church membership, encouraging the members of the Church "as individual citizens to promote efforts in the civil sphere to restrict abortion on demand by statute." This was adopted after a floor fight on a substitute resolution urging cooperation with other groups seeking to pass a constitutional amendment prohibiting abortion on demand, which was defeated by the Congress General Assembly. The committee's focus was clearly on the local level. The only new element in its report was a call for the preparation by "a select group of qualified persons to be commissioned by the Archdiocese to prepare position papers, presenting the Greek Orthodox position on social and moral issues." There followed a very impressive list of twenty-five topics, one of which had five sub-topics. The request seemed to acknowledge that local level social and moral concern activity could be genuinely promoted only if firm direction and guidance was to come from the official church.

On the surface, Chicago did not do much. Yet, it seems clear that this congress had assumed a mature and realistic view of the situation. It recognized instinctively that the localization of social and moral concerns needed preparation in terms of consciousness raising, application to the internal life of parishes of these values, as well as firm, clear-cut moral and spiritual direction on a wide range of issues. It would appear that the convener, Bishop Soterios of Toronto; the chairman, Attorney John Plumides; and consultants, Rev. Constantine Volaitis; and religious journalist, James Couchell, had understood the situation to demand a tactical response, and the report reflected that understanding. The movement from hierarchical inspiration and direction-giving, to national forum pronouncement, though impressive, was easily accomplished compared with the task of local acceptance. Five-hundred years of imposed inward orientation under the Turkish domination would not be reversed easily.[9]

The Bicentennial celebration of the United States of America found the Greek Orthodox Archdiocese—always sensitive to the symbolic—in Philadelphia, Pennsylvania, on the 4th of July, fully involved in the work of the 23rd Clergy-Laity Congress. Held between July 2 and 9, 1976 the Congress included observances of Independence Day as well as a parade on July 7, which involved 1,000 young adults and teenagers of the Church.

The two years between Chicago and Philadelphia saw some important progress. An office of Inter-Church Relations and Social Concerns was established. It remains functioning to the present. Appointed to the dual ecumenical and social position was the former dean of Holy Cross Greek Orthodox School of Theology, Rev. Nicon D. Patrinacos. His contribution to the work of the committee was most significant. In accordance with the directives of the 22nd Clergy-Laity Congress, a beginning was made in addressing some of the 25 (or 29, depending upon how the report was read) topics. From the list, Fr. Patrinacos prepared four position papers and also addressed a topic not on the list. Chosen for treatment were abortion, birth control, drinking and alcoholism, homosexuality and the new topic, the danger of community over-expansion. It was indicated in the report[10] that Father Patrinacos had written first drafts, that the committee had refined and developed them, and that they were presented "for the purpose of providing guidelines for our communicants." The committee made the point that the statements should "not be taken as being in the nature of theological pronouncements," though they were presented as "being in accordance with Orthodox theology and tradition." Father Patrinacos served as a consultant to the committee which was chaired by Bishop Gerasimos of Abydos, with Mr. Evan Chris Alevizatos as rapporteur.

The form of the statements was interesting and quite understandable from the point of view of the purpose of committee—they consisted of one-sentence paragraphs, each preceded by a small dot or period. Thus, the first three of ten one-sentence paragraphs on the topic of abortion read as follows:

> The Orthodox Church has a definite, formal and expressed attitude toward abortion. It condemns all positive procedures purporting to abort the embryo or fetus, whether by surgical or by chemical means. The Orthodox Church brands abortion as muder; that is, as a premeditated termination of the life of a human being.

In the same style it continues to deal with genetic questions, the issue of the threatened life of the mother, legal decisions and the practice of Christians regarding abortion.

The birth control position paper speaks of the traditional prohibitions of birth control and proceeds to legitimatize family spacing of children, rejecting the complete avoidance of child-bearing, discussing the means appropriate to birth control, the purposes of marriage and the purpose of sexual relations in marriage.

The position paper on drinking-alcoholism, following the same one-sentence paragraph format, seeks to provide for control of "habitual drinking." The models provided by parents for their children is a major concern. The report holds that habitual drinking leads to alcoholism. The proper response to the tensions which lead persons to the "temporary absence from reality" caused by intoxication," is to be found in a new view and approach of experience by way of reclaiming our divine sonship." Alcoholism, itself, however, is approached as a disease, arising primarily, but not exclusively, from disturbed personalities. The way of repentance; leading to an inward return "to the source of real and lasting power, which is God's love for man" is advised along with medical and psychological help.

The longest, most carefully reasoned and analyzed topic in this report is on homosexuality. It is a strong rebuttal, couched mainly in psychological language, of the trends which promote the idea of homosexuality as a morally acceptable alternative life-style. More than any other, this report of the Congress's Social and Moral Issues Committee is replete with technical, psychological, sociological, and theological terminology. It is seen as a moral problem, as well. It refuses to consider the marriage of homosexuals as appropriate to Orthodox Christian views. In the end, it tries to develop a measure of compassionate understanding of the situation of the homosexually inclined person, but the general tone is put in very strong negative terms.

The final topic, "The Dangers of Community Over-Expansion," reverts to more simple and to more religious language. But it does not lose its psychological orientation completely. It charges that the tendency to commit future parish resources to ambitious building programs may have its real source in moral pride or in shallow and self-deceiving spirituality. The last two paragraphs outline the deleterious impact which community over-expansion may have:

> No beautiful churches and no imposing community buildings can balance the loss of love in a community. What would a Greek Orthodox community profit if it "won the whole world, but lost its soul?"

The report was completely oriented toward the parish and individual life of the Church. Its pronouncements, made in quite strong language, were directed inward, and only by implication could a message for a public social stance be seen. This trend would continue on to the next Clergy-Laity Congress.

The 24th Clergy-Laity Congress was held from July 1 through July 7, 1978 in Detroit, Michigan. On the last day of the congress, the Social and Moral Issues Committee made its report. It was not a report of strong new moves, but sought to reaffirm the positions taken in Philadelphia two years before, including opposition to abortion and to the legalization of homosexual behavior. It also "requested that the Archdiocese implement the resolution on all forms of gambling (bingo, other games of chance, etc.) in the parish, as it was adopted in Chicago, 1974."[11] Once again, the Social and Moral Issues called for "the formulation of position papers," understood as "concise statements as guidelines...to be presented during the 1980 Clergy-Laity Congress."[12] The list of topics called for was wide-ranging. It included the following fifteen topics: 1. divorce; 2. interfaith marriages; 3. child abuse; 4. pornography; 5. human rights; 6. equal rights; 7. euthanasia–death and dying; 8. donation of organs after death; 9. arms race–disarmaments; 10. cremation; 11. criminal justice; 12. abortion; 13. embryo fertilization outside the womb; 14. homosexuality; 15. transexuals.

The Archdiocese acted quickly and assigned the topics to the faculty of Holy Cross Greek Orthodox School of Theology. Dean Stanley S. Harakas assumed personal responsibility for the project which became a topic of study in his social ethics classes taught at the School. By the subsequent Clergy-Laity Congress, held in 1980 in Atlanta, Georgia, the first drafts of the position papers were ready for the committee to discuss.

One way of viewing the work of the Social and Moral Issues Committee of 1978 is to see it as resuming the two-prong apaproach of both outward concern and parish social and moral responsibility. It also was directing itself to the need for the development of a social ethic which could be something more than a press release. The demand for a theologically grounded set of positions indicated increasing seriousness regarding the involvement of the Church in this area of Christian outreach. The convener of the 1978 Social and Moral Issues Committee was, once again, Bishop Meletios (Tripodakis) of Christianoupolis; chairman was James Papadakis of Rocky River, Ohio; and secretary was the Very Reverend Eugene Pappas of Omaha, Nebraska, formerly a missionary priest in Korea.

Of additional interest were the large number of resolutions passed by this congress of social and moral issues topics, a sure sign that the appropriateness and propriety of the involvement of the Church in such topics was generally accepted at the congress. Thus, it called for Jerusalem to be designated an "open city"; opposed the view of President Carter that the Turkish arms embargo be lifted; called for a resumption of peace talks in the Middle East; approved "wholeheartedly" the Supreme Court decision on the "seven dirty words" case which prohibits the broadcasting of offensive language; issued a "call to action" inviting all churches and synagogues to join together to fight "atheism, Marxist dialectics, eudaemonism, and hedonism" as well as "every movement that violates and annihilates human rights. . ." It further called on all international agencies and religious groups and leaders to attend to unjust restrictions and constraints placed on the Ecumenical Patriarchate by the Turkish government. In addition, it called for support of earthquake victims in Thessalonike, Greece, and support of the programs of the U.N. "Year of the Child." Significantly it sent three letters to President Carter, the first of which expressed grave concern about the escalation of the arms race and the threat this "poses to the peace of the world." The second declared that it is

the right and duty of all Americans to disagree with America's foreign policy when they believe it to be unwise and detrimental to the advancement of American interest and incompatible with the rule of law and the principles of justice, morality and honor upon which our nation was founded.

Certainly this was an act which hardly fit the Caesaropapist view widely believed to be held by the Orthodox. It was not, in fact without precedent, either in the distant or the recent past of the Orthodox Church. The third letter was one of praise and support for the President's human rights policies.[14]

Of additional interest was the report of the Congress Philoptochos Society Committee. (The Philoptochos is the women's organization of the Church, whose name means "friends of the poor.") The National Philoptochos met concurrently with the Clergy-Laity Congress. It was reported that for the first time "a Philoptochos convention concerned itself with social and moral issues through a panel composed of five members exploring the following subjects: right to life/abortion; church and family; sex education in the schools; the selling of liquor/games of chance; the abused child; ordination of women; battered women/child abuse." It was recorded that spirited discussion followed the presentations.[15]

The decisions of the 25th Clergy-Laity Congress held in Atlanta, Georgia, from June 24 to July 4, 1980 were officially published late in 1981. The committee did do some important work which is not reported in detail in the official proceedings and which needs to be reported here.

Its major task was to review and comment upon the fifteen position papers presented to it as a result of the decisions of the previous congress. Feeling that certain issues touched upon in the position papers needed to be stressed, the committee made certain recommendations to the congress. These referred to the establishment of programs to work against divorce; it emphasized the freedom of worship as the most basic human right; it supported the idea behind the proposed Equal Rights Amendment; it expressed the sentiment that it was strongly opposed to the broadening of the arms race; it articulated support, regarding abortion, for efforts to promulgate and implement legislation which is intended to protect human life upon its conception, as a fundamental right of all humanity; and, it called for the selection of parish council members based on qualities which include spiritual criteria.

In addition, the Moral and Social Issues Committee of the 25th Clergy-Laity Congress is reported to have called for the preparation of additional position papers on the following topics: stewardship, birth control and sterilization, conscientious objection, sects, capital punishment, spouse and parental abuse, the effect of media on society and values, and nuclear energy.[16]

The committee did not bring the fifteen position papers to the floor. The texts, with a record of the committee responses and suggested corrections, additions and deletions were, subsequent to the congress, translated into Modern Greek and submitted to the Greek Orthodox Archdiocese Synod of Bishops for formal consideration. Once discussed and voted upon by the synod, the position papers will be submitted to the Ecumenical Patrariarchate for ratification. At that time they will become formal policy of the Greek Orthodox Archdiocese. In this manner will theology, the consciousness of the body of Christ, and the teaching authority of the episcopate all have had their input in the formulation and development of these documents.

The report of the committee of the 1980 Clergy-Laity Congress was handled in a way which hisitory may some day come to call 'transitional.' The report was debated on the floor and modified. In some cases the modification came directly from the floor. In other cases, it was accomplished by a reworking by the committee between sessions so as to account for objections. The congress passed a statement of equal rights, for instance, which stopped short of endorsing the proposed Equal Rights Amendment, but used the words of the amendment. In part is said, "Accordingly we believe and support the proposition that equality of rights shall not be denied or abridged under the terms of any law solely because of sex."

The committee statement on disarmament was also modified by a floor substitution so that the position taken was made significantly more cautious. It called for a method which would insure "that all mankind would be served," so that all of humanity would not "be at the mercy" of one or a few world powers, and that disarmament should not occur through a defeatist attitude."[18]

The whole report was then adopted, and it was announced by the Archbishop that the report would be sent to the Synod of

Bishops "for study and then forwarded, together with its findings to the Ecumenical Patriarchate."[19]

In addition to the report of the Social and Moral Issues Committee, the congress issued resolutions and statements many of which were oriented toward social concerns. Some of these cannot but be characterized as political in the narrow sense of the term. Thus, the resolutions on the Ecumenical Patriarchate, the American Hostages, the resolution on the Armed Occupation of Cyprus and the resolution on Peace in the Aegean, expressed the concerns of the Greek Orthodox people who made up the congress on what have now become clearly political concerns, though, of course, couched in the right language appropriate to the Church. A significant and important resolution on Human and Religious Rights followed. It called upon regimes which oppressed people, "to insure the free and unhindered exercise of these vital rights to all citizens regardless of racial or ethnic origin, or political or religious espousal." It also called on the democratic nations to adopt, "clear, concise and consistent policies, both domestic and foreign, reflective of these fundamental human rights."[20] Further, a resolution on Peace and Disarmament was issued which called for "the leaders of all nations to exert every effort to de-escalate the arms race, and to work ceaselessly toward the goal of peace."[21]

In addition, statements and resolutions were issued on Jerusalem (that it become a "free city"); on Third World needs (the prosperous of the world to render moral support and material assistance to third world peoples); on support for a "responsible energy Sabbath"; on the family (opposition to those forces which foster child abuse, the 'new morality,' the living-together style of life, the 'gay' movement and abortion) and support for whatever supports and safeguards the high moral standards of the Christian family); on religious freedom, on moral and social issues; on morality in international relations; and on marriage and the family. In all, the 1980 Clergy-Laity Congress assumed a strong and wide-ranging stance on moral and social issues. It was, in a sense, a coming of age by the Orthodox Church and yet, the beginning of a new *modus operandi* in the formation of social and moral positions by reference to the Synod of Bishops for ultimate ecclesial authority. This method continues to involve clergy, laity, theology, and hierarchy, but offers a vehicle for a more 'official' articulation of Church views while continuing the contribution of representatives of the whole Church.

A final thing needs to be noted about the decisions of the 25th

Clergy-Laity Congress Social and Moral Issues Committee: its balance between concern with issues of public policy and concern with issues focusing on the moral and spiritual life of the members of the Orthodox Church. Such a balanced approach cannot help but auger well for the future treatment of these issues. The convener was Bishop Anthony of San Francisco; chairing the committee was Attorney Elenie Huszagh; and resource person was the Reverend Stanley S. Harakas.

A Cross Reference to Moral and Social Issues in the Clergy-Laity Congress Reports and Congress Resolutions

There follows a partial cross reference to social and moral issues as addressed by the Clergy-Laity Congresses from the 17th Clergy-Laity Congress (1964) to the 25th Congress held in 1980.

1. *Parish Oriented Decisions*

a) Social and Moral Issues in Parish Life

21st Clergy-Laity Congress — 1972
22nd Clergy-Laity Congress — 1974
23rd Clergy-Laity Congress — 1976
24th Clergy-Laity Congress — 1978
25th Clergy-Laity Congress — 1980

b) Church and Spiritual Issues

18th Clergy-Laity Congress — 1966

c) Individual Employment and Orthodox Identity

21st Clergy-Laity Congress — 1972

d) Fundraising

22nd Clergy-Laity Congress — 1974

e) Immigration

19th Clergy-Laity Congress — 1968

2. *Social Concern Organization and Implementation*

a) Social Consciousness Development

21st Clergy-Laity Congress — 1972
22nd Clergy-Laity Congress — 1974
24th Clergy-Laity Congress — 1978

b) Office of Social Concerns

20th Clergy-Laity Congress — 1970
21st Clergy-Laity Congress — 1972

c) Social Action

18th Clergy-Laity Congress – 1966
24th Clergy-Laity Congress – 1978

3. *Issues Primarily Concerned With Public Morality*

a) Moral Disintegration – Secularism

18th Clergy-Laity Congress – 1966
19th Clergy-Laity Congress – 1968
21st Clergy-Laity Congress – 1972

b) Civil Rights – Race Relations – Underprivileged

17th Clergy-Laity Congress – 1964
18th Clergy-Laity Congress – 1966
20th Clergy-Laity Congress – 1970
21st Clergy-Laity Congress – 1972
25th Clergy-Laity Congress – 1980

c) Women's Concerns

21st Clergy-Laity Congress – 1972
25th Clergy-Laity Congress – 1980

d) Human Rights/Human Dignity

18th Clergy-Laity Congress – 1966
19th Clergy-Laity Congress – 1968
24th Clergy-Laity Congress – 1978
25th Clergy-Laity Congress – 1980

e) Family Life

18th Clergy-Laity Congress – 1966
21st Clergy-Laity Congress – 1972
24th Clergy-Laity Congress – 1978
25th Clergy-Laity Congress – 1980

f) Pornography

20th Clergy-Laity Congress – 1970
24th Clergy-Laity Congress – 1978

g) Homosexuality

21st Clergy-Laity Congress – 1972
23rd Clergy-Laity Congress – 1976
24th Clergy-Laity Congress – 1978

h) Abortion

20th Clergy-Laity Congress – 1970
22nd Clergy-Laity Congress – 1974
23rd Clergy-Laity Congress – 1976
24th Clergy-Laity Congress – 1978

25th Clergy-Laity Congress — 1980

i) Alcoholism and Drug Abuse

18th Clergy-Laity Congress — 1966
20th Clergy-Laity Congress — 1970
23rd Clergy-Laity Congress — 1976
24th Clergy-Laity Congress — 1978

j) Crime and Juvenile Delinquency

18th Clergy-Laity Congress — 1966
19th Clergy-Laity Congress — 1968
20th Clergy-Laity Congress — 1970
21st Clergy-Laity Congress — 1972

k) World Peace — War — Arms Race

18th Clergy-Laity Congress — 1966
19th Clergy-Laity Congress — 1968
20th Clergy-Laity Congress — 1970
21st Clergy-Laity Congress — 1972
24th Clergy-Laity Congress — 1978
25th Clergy-Laity Congress — 1980

l) Civil Disobedience — The Draft and The Law

19th Clergy-Laity Congress — 1968
21st Clergy-Laity Congress — 1972

m) Mass Media

19th Clergy-Laity Congress — 1968

n) Ecology

20th Clergy-Laity Congress — 1970
25th Clergy-Laity Congress — 1980

The texts to these decisions will be found in the following chapter.

Notes

1. All references in this chapter refer to the texts collected in Chapter 5 entitled "The Social and Moral Issues Committee Reports of the Clergy-Laity Congress."

2. Charles C. Moskos, Jr., *Greek-Americans: Struggle and Success.* (New York, 1980). Moskos notes that Greek-Americans in general have presented an unusual pattern for immigrant groups in the U.S.A. while assimilation has taken place quite rapidly (i.e., entrance into institutional structures of the nation), acculturation (i.e., aquisition of norms and behavior patterns) has not. This has served to create a "in the nation but not *of* the nation" mentality, a striking phenomenon, when viewed from the perspective of Christian Social Ethics categories.

3. *Decisions and Resolutions: 17th Biennial Clergy-Laity Congress of the Greek*

Orthodox Archdiocese of North and South America. Denver, Colorado, June 28th-July 3rd, 1964 (New York, n.d.), pp. 37-41.

4. *Decisions and Resolutions: 18th Biennial Clergy-Laity Congress of the Greek Orthodox Archdiocese of North and South America. Montreal, Quebec, Canada, June 25th-July 2nd, 1966* (New York, n.d.), separate pagination pp. 1-5.

5. Πρακτικά τῆς 'Εν 'Αθήναις (20-27 'Ιουλίου, 1968) ΙΘ' Κληρικολαϊκῆς Συνελεύσεως τῆς Κοινοτήτων τῆς 'Ελληνικῆς 'Ορθοδόξου 'Αρχιεπίσκοπης Βορείου καί Νοτίου 'Αμερικῆς (New York, n.d.), pp. 68-73.

6. *Decisions of the 20th Clergy-Laity Congress of the Greek Orthodox Archdiocese of North and South America in New York, June 28th-July 4th, 1970* (New York, n.d.), pp. 66-70.

7. *Decisions of the 21st Clergy-Laity Congress of the Greek Orthodox Archdiocese of North and South America in Houston, Texas, July 1st-7th, 1972* (New York, n.d.), pp. 63-70.

8. *Decisions of the 22nd Clergy-Laity Congress of the Greek Orthodox Archdiocese of North and South America in Chicago, Illinois, June 30th-July 7th, 1974* (New York, n.d.), pp. 92-95

9. The topics for which position papers were to have been written were the following: 1) The moral crisis in the nation; 2) euthanasia; 3) war, peace; 4) evolution; 5) the right to life, abortion; 6) contraception and sterilization; 7) aid to parochial schools; 8) drug abuse; 9) the family, divorce, mixed marriages; 10) venereal diseases; 11) gambling, fundraising methods; 12) alcoholism; 13) capital punishment; 14) penal reform; 15) equal opportunity for human development, a. minority groups, b. women, c. busing, d. newly arrived immigrants, e. senior citizens; 16) freedom of the press; 17) religious liberty; 18) pornography; 19) secularization of society; 20) amnesty; 21) the Church and its relation to civil authority; 22) the Church and social activism; 23) homosexuality; 24) prostitution; 25) multi-culturism and multi-lingualism.

10. *Decisions of the 23rd Clergy-Laity Congress of the Greek Orthodox Archdiocese of North and South America. New York: Greek Orthodox Archdiocese of North and South America* (New York, n.d.), pp. 98-102.

11. *Congress Newsrelease*, Detroit, Michigan, July 7, 1978, Archdiocesan Archives, p. 1.

12. *Ibid.*, pp. 1, 2.

13. *Decisions of the 24th Clergy-Laity Congress of the Greek Orthodox Archdiocese of North and South America. Detroit, Michigan, July 1st-7th, 1978* (New York, n.d.), pp. 94-95. This list differs from the listing in the public relations release, as well from the list finally published in the official acts of the Congress, both in number of topics and in specific topics. The list reproduced here is from the letter of the Archdiocese assigning the topics to the Holy Cross Theological School for treatment. Not on this list as published above in the text, but in the listing as published in the *Decisions* were "Inter-Orthodox marriage," and "Marriage outside the church of faith." On the list used to prepare the position papers, but not on the *Decisions* list were abortion and homosexuality, deleted perhaps, because statements had already been prepared and two other issues, "Embryo fertilization outside the womb," and "Transexuals."

14. *Ibid.*, pp. 101-08.

15. *Ibid.*, pp. 99-101.

16. This account is based on the *Orthodox Observer* article, "A Summary...Congress Reports." *Orthodox Observer*, Vol. 46, No. 847, August 13, 1980, pp. 1, 3.

17. *Minutes, Decisions, Resolutions, and Statements of the 25th Clergy-Laity Congress of the Greek Orthodox Archdiocese of North and South America in Atlanta, Georgia, June 27-July 5, 1980*, p. 90.

18. *Ibid.*

19. *Ibid.*, p. 91.

20. *Ibid.*, p. 115.

21. *Ibid.*, p. 116.

Chapter Five

THE SOCIAL AND MORAL ISSUES COMMITTEE REPORTS OF THE CLERGY-LAITY CONGRESSES

I know from personal experience that the suggestion was first made to establish a committee on social and moral issues at the 13th Clergy-Laity Congress held in Washington, D. C. from 30 September to 6 October 1956. However, a decade was to pass before the committee was to be established at the 18th Clergy-Laity Congress in Montreal. Yet there is a pre-history of the committee which ought not to be ignored.

The Pre-History of the Social and Moral Issues Committees

Very little can be discerned in the 1954 12th Clergy-Laity Congress report that relates to our topic. There is a report on philanthropy which catalogues donations to charities (notably the Ionian Earthquake Relief) by the Archdiocese,[1] but there is little else. The 13th Clergy-Laity Congress, mentioned above, had a very short list of "Decisions and Resolutions." Among the later were "brotherly greetings to all of our fellow Americans, irrespective of race, creed or social status," with the purpose of urging them "to cooperate with one another in the true spirit of complete understanding and Christian brotherhood for the solution of the problems facing us."[2] Other resolutions were made with reference to Communism, religion and culture, the U.S. Constitution, and immigration laws.

The first Clergy-Laity Congress over which Archbishop Iakovos presided issued resolutions which were limited to the internal concerns and affairs of the Archdiocese: Education and Greek Letters; Administration; Finances; The Mixed Council; Philoptochos Society; Youth, etc.[3] All these, in one form or another have been perennial topics of the Clergy-Laity Congresses. However, not even a single line can be associated with social and moral issues. However, appended to the Resolutions was the text of "an official statement on aims and purposes" which was to prove-in-fact an outline of the emphases which the Archbishop was to focus upon during the subsequent years of his tenure. In general, the seven points look outward. The first is clearly pertinent to our subject. For the sake of the record, the text of the official statement, derived from the

15th Clergy-Laity Congress in Buffalo, New York, is cited below.

Archbishop Iakovos' Message to the Press

1. The 15th Congress, just concluded, provided the Greek Orthodox Church with a deeper understanding of its mission which is to exert to its fullest extent its spiritual, cultural and moral influence in America. The members of the Church are committed to combating all phases of current social evil prevalent today, such as Communism, juvenile delinquency, crime, indecent literature, the abuse of liquor, and gambling.

2. For the first time a Congress of the Church expressed the full determination of its membership to work with every other Church in America, which sincerely wishes to bear witness to the observance of moral order and to the strengthening of our society with deeper spiritual values.

3. The Church is more than ever eager to effect a closer approachment with the Roman Catholic Church and with all Protestant groups that are dedicated to the promotion of the ecumenical movement for Christian unity, in the hope that the day will come when the Orthodox Chruch, which is giving a great witness to its faith, may do so in unison with all Christian Churches and with greater courage.

4. We adhere most faithfully to the democratic principles of our country and express our determination to fully support the policies of our government for the securing of the peace of the world and justice.

5. In reflection of the sentiments of the Congress on religious issues, our Church declares that it is inconsistent with our history to deviate from the fullest possible discharge of service to our country, by creating other issues which will divert our best contribution to our country and to humanity.

6. We believe our nation will be second to none in the race to conquer space, and that it is, undoubtedly, the only nation, in cooperation with its freedom-loving allies, that is moved in all its actions by ultimate faith in God and His divine will.

7. We have prayed during this Congress, as organized atheism is waging a battle relentlessly against God and peace, that Almighty God will inspire all the leaders of the free world and all nations, with the realization that lasting peace is attainable only through the prevalence of humility, love and obedience to the divine will and law.[4]

The 17th Clergy-Laity Congress held in Denver, Colorado, in 1964 issued a short list of "recommendations and resolutions."[5] Included were "A protest regarding the persecution of the Ecumenical Patriarchate and Greek Minority in Turkey," and a resolution "Regarding reiteration of loyalty and devotion to America." There was also a significant resolution on Civil Rights, affirming at once the evils of racial segregation while also opposing violence. As a first offering in the area of social concern by a Clergy-Laity Congress of the Greek Archdiocese it is significant.

Regarding Civil Rights

WHEREAS, the Standing Conference of Canonical Orthodox Bishops in the Americas, has issued an official statement on Civil Rights in the United States of America, stating:

The Standing Conference of Canonical Orthodox Bishops in an official meeting on Friday, the twenty-fourth day of April, in the year nineteen hundred and sixty four, in the city of New York, gives praise to God for the majesty of His Kingdom and the blessing of His mercies which so abundantly grace our land.

Throughout the ages, the Orthodox Church has survived centuries of persecution which, even to this day, continues to be imposed upon untold millions of Orthodox Christians in many lands. The Orthodox Church has borne the yoke of oppression and is wholly aware that persecution, prejudice and intolerance is the greatest sin that the free soul of man can bear. We, therefore, extend and join with our fellow Christians and citizens everywhere in deploring all vestiges of segregation that deny to free men, the dignity of equal rights. We pray that the spirit of compassion, patience, and understanding brotherhood will penetrate the hearts of all men and women whose leadership must guide the destiny of the great racial challenge facing America.

As children of God made in His image, we urge that all men of all races exercise disciplined restraint in declaring their God-given beliefs and rights so that these blessings may be freely gained in a society which constitutionally and spiritually guarantees these rights.

The Church deplores violence, but upholds the right of free men and women to act as the People of God in expressing their rights to the God-given principles which no man can be denied because of color or creed. The power of love is the power of God, and as God is *Love*, so love is the greatest power of His Children

on earth. We prayerfully beseech our fellow citizens, and especially the leaders of our nation, to direct their actions with the
power of love as their beacon of eternal hope, a hope which will
not be denied in an America which will give to all men, the example of his Word. We pray that all men may transcend the limitations of human fraility, and as God-fearing Christians and dedicated Americans, transmit the spirit of prayer of our Lord and
Savior, Jesus Christ: "Thy Will be done on earth as it is in Heaven."

BE IT RESOLVED THAT, the Delegates to the Seventeenth Biennial Congress of the Greek Orthodox Archdiocese of North
and South America gathered here in the city of Denver, Colorado,
this first day of July in the year nineteen hundred and sixty four
do hereby reaffirm the above statement. [6]

These efforts and emphases, led finally to the establishment of a
regularly constituted Clergy-Laity Congress Committee on Social
and Moral Issues. The purpose of this chapter is not to analyze or
study the texts of these reports, but only to present the material
for further study. We make these reports available to the public
in this place in order to document the interest of the Clergy-Laity
Congresses in subjects of moral and social concern.

However, it must be noted that there is a disparity of style, subject matter and even — to a measure — of moral stance on these issues.
This is due to the fact that various persons had positions of influence on these committees as constituted at each of the Congresses.
They also reflect the tensions in the thinking of the Orthodox on
social issues. It will be left to future studies to delineate these. However, their value for the discipline of Orthodox Christian ethics is
important.

From the 18th through the 23rd Congresses, we simply provide
the texts of the reports of the Social and Moral Issues Committee,
as well as other pertinent Clergy-Laity Congress reports, without
comment.

THE TEXTS

18TH CLERGY-LAITY CONGRESS, 1966, MONTREAL

Committee on the Church, and the Moral and Social Issues of our Time

As the Greek Orthodox Church in the Americas takes her place in the mainstream of the 20th Century, she does so with full devotion to the consciousness of her nature as the One, Holy, Catholic and Apostolic Church of Jesus Christ, and by manifesting her centuries-long concern with the physical, moral and spiritual needs of the whole man and the whole of society. It is toward the fulfillment of these needs, as expressed in the contemporary social and moral problems of this age, that this Committee addresses its concern as follows:

Human Rights: The Bible declares that, "God created man in His own image and likeness" (Gen.1.27), and the Christian Church accordingly reaffirms that all men are created equal. It is the profound concern of the Church that discrimination in all forms be eradicated, and we appeal to our parishes and people to stand steadfast in the protection of individual human rights, particularly in such areas as employment, housing, education and hospitalization. This Clergy-Laity Congress commends His Eminence Archbishop Iakovos for the leadership and direction he has given to the Greek Orthodox Church in the movement of human rights.

World Peace: The Greek Orthodox Church recognizes the God-given right of all men to live a life of dignity in peace. However, the sad lessons of history reveal that the peace of Christ has always demanded a long and relentless struggle, and the forces of evil in our own day, as in the past, are adamant in destroying that peace. The eternal commitment of the Greek Orthodox Church to the cause of world peace will not permit it to ignore the suffering and oppression of our fellowmen, and, therefore, wholly supports America's commitment to the pursuit of peace in Viet Nam. We deplore however, such hypocritical acts of pacifism as draft-card burning and the evasion of military service, for we affirm that freedom is not and has never been totally free. The preservation of our cherished rights and liberties requires the solemn obligation and duties of citizenship among which the Church recognizes as most important, the service to and defense of country in time of need.

Moral Disintegration: Man's record today bears irrefutable evidence of widespread moral and spiritual disintegration, and some of the major contributing sources to this disintegration are reflected in such areas as:

1. Man's obsession with the material aspects of life which has penetrated every social class and led to a confusion of values.

2. The breaking down of family life as expressed in the lack of regard for the sacramental character of marriage and the failure of parents to provide proper leadership in the upbringing of children.

3. A misinterpretation of the principle of the separation of Church and State to wrongly mean the alienation of religion from public life.

4. The apathy, indifference and hypocrisy of many Church members, which contributes to their unwittingly condoning and encouraging disrespect for moral law.

We, therefore, call upon the clergy and lay leaders of our communities to formulate parish programs which will help curb such disintegration, and to actively join forces with other concerned persons, organizations, and societies who are likewise combating the social evils and immorality.

Crime and Juvenile Delinquency: We recognize that the alarming increase of crime and juvenile delinquency is weakening the sinews of our society. It well-known that family structure among the Greek Orthodox emphasizes self respect, discipline, pride, obedience and respect for authority. We ought, therefore, to cultivate this inherent family strength and encourage these qualities which contribute to strong family life in society. We urge our parish leaders to participate in community agencies and programs dedicated to combating crime and juvenile delinquency, and to avail parish facilities to assist such endeavors. The participation in such public programs as the annual observance of Law Day on May 1st will give added stature and public recognition to the need for respect of law and good citizenship. In short, we reaffirm the eloquence of President Abraham Lincoln whose immortal description of respect for the law we paraphrase: "Let reverence for the law become the political religion of the nation."

Alcoholism and Narcotics: The Greek Orthodox Church is cognizant of its moral responsibility to those suffering from alcoholism and narcotics addiction. Although the moderate use of alcohol is not condemned by the Church, it is keenly recognized that overindulgence creates potential alcoholics. We, therefore, call upon the clergy and communicants of the Greek Orthodox Church to arrest these widespread social ravages, and to aid and cooperate with all social services working towards this end.

The Underprivileged: The Greek Orthodox Church has always been in the forefront of the struggle to protect the poor and the weak in fighting illiteracy and social neglect. We are called upon in these days to expand our concept of Orthodox Christian devotion to charity to include a concern for those of our fellow-citizens who are economically, socially, and educationally underprivileged, for it is the prayer of the Church that poverty may, in our lifetime, be speedily and effectively eradicated. The Church recognizes that all persons are entitled to equal treatment and opportunity. However, the large problem areas of the underprivileged can only be handled by governmental concern.

Social Action: In order that the foregoing areas of social concern be continued, directed and expanded, we strongly recommend that there be established in the Archdiocese a Department of Social Action, and that each local parish establish a Social Action Committee under the direction of the parish priest and parish council.

Committee on the Church and Spiritual Issues

The charge of this Committee was to study some of the spiritual issues and problems that face the contemporary church. In its solving of these problems the Committee took cognizance of several major factors that directly contribute toward this dilemma. These are as follows:

1. A lack of full understanding by most laymen of the true mission of the Church.

2. The danger of increasing secularism which threatens the fundamental spiritual goals and concepts of the Church.

3. The dichotomy of religion and culture which is alien to Orthodoxy and creates increasing spiritual problems.

Toward the solution of such enormous challenges this Committee offered three observations:

First: that solutions to such all-encompassing problems require a basic cognizance that these problems do exist, but that immediate and final answers cannot and should not be readily expected.

Second: that toward their solution a commission be appointed to study and implement the establishment of a lay apostolate for deeper involvement and renewal of the laity into the total and inner life of the Church.

Third: The establishment of centers of Orthodox studies for the systematic presentation and transmission of our Orthodox Faith.

Committee on Church and Family

The family is the holiest of God's institutions in the world, and the bond that exists betweeen man and woman, created by Him since Creation and surrounded by divine authority, has thus become everlasting and undissolved for eternity.

The family is the spiritual kingdom of God that was established in the Garden of Eden. It thereby entered into history and will continue its life and existence for eternity.

After "the fulfillment of time" Jesus Christ was born, became man, and presents the ideal family as personified by the "Family of Nazareth"; the "Family of Cana"; and the "Family of Bethany," which by example establishes the position of each family member: the position of the man as the head of the woman as "Jesus Christ is the head of the Church" (Eph 5.23); the position of the woman "who is subject to the man" (Eph 5.24); the position of children, who are those who are the beloved inheritors of God's Kingdom (Mat. 19:14); and the position of the Christian family which is based upon being worthy of God's bounty as they live and function according to His will.

The moral and spiritual crisis in both the family and society is great, and the reasons for this crisis are: A rejection of moral principles, expecially the fundamental Christian principles of faith and love; the denial of Greek Orthodox family traditions, and a lack of loyalty and concern for the home by members of the family; the absence of spiritual unity in the home; the indifference of parents toward their children and a denial of faithfulness to Christ, His teachings and His Church.

The clergy and laity of the Church have an unprecedented responsibility in facing the challenge of the great moral crisis which confronts the world. To save the family from further deterioration is a challenge of sobering dimension, and the joint mission of the clergy and laity is to guide the family towards Christ because there is only one, *Jesus Christ*, the absolute savior of the family (Acts 4.12) for only through Jesus Christ will the family find continuing joy, happiness and peace on earth and in heaven (Gal. 5.22).

It is necessary that we emphasize to all, expecially our youth, that a marriage without faith and self-sacrifice, virtue and Christ, is a structure without foundation. It is, therefore, with the seal of the Word of God that we complete this presentation with the promise rendered to us from the Epistle of St. Timothy: "Godliness is profitable unto all things, having promise of the life that now is, and of that which is to come" (1 Timothy 4:8).

19TH CLERGY-LAITY CONGRESS. 1968, ATHENS, GREECE

Moral and Social Issues Committee

Relevance—Secularism

After the fall of Troy, the citizens were allowed to take one object which they valued the most from their homes. A young man, Aenias, entered his home and emerged carrying the statue of his god. When the conquerors saw this, they were moved, and they told him to return and remove another object whereupon he reentered to carry out on his back his aged father.

In Columbus, Ohio, a severe flood took place recently displacing thousands from their homes. T. V. newsmen asked these persons what they had first removed from their homes. The answer of most: their TV sets. These two accounts demonstrate so graphically the change in values that have taken place in our times.

The wave of secularism which stands as the greatest danger, threat and at the same time, the greatest challenge to the Christian Church, stands as the underlying cause of every social and political ill of modern man, whether it be crime in the streets, narcotics, war, high divorce rates, broken homes, alcoholism, or civil disorders. Secularism, regretfully, is the tragic offspring of schism, the final harvest of theological distortion that began with Augustine in the 4th century and had its full flowering in the Renaissance. The gods have fled from the secular city and modern man remains alone, uprooted and isolated. Western man believes only in his own powers, his own abilities, in his own capacity to alter and control destiny. Instead of God, he worships only the distorted demonic image of his own self. Modern man, like a new prodigal, finds himself off in a far country, that tragic place where God is not.

The greatest single task facing the Christian world today is to make the great central truths of the Christian faith relevant to today's man, in terms that are meaningful in day-to-day relationships and which would place these relationships under a new light which gives them new dimensions of depth and richness, thereby transforming life.

This involves a new expression of our theology that avoids the distortions of medieval western theology and is simultaneously a return to the spirit of the fathers of the church, where theology and life are very closely linked. Language problems have to be dealt with honestly and intelligently on several levels. The meanings of words change and those terms that have become cliches and platitudes must be redefined so that they again may be conveyors of ideas. Translations must glow and vibrate rather than stifle and dullen. Translation into an idiom that is understandable is an unqualified prerequisite for any church that is even in the least concerned with the problem of relevance. Translation is not the whole answer, but it is an integral, indispensable part of any search for meaning. Within the Holy Scriptures, contemporary man can find vital, exciting and transforming ideas that many times have been adapted by modern science as new, novel, and as their own particular discoveries. When we speak of a liturgical experience, we must emphasize that worship is the culmination, not the beginning of man's spiritual odyssey. Man cannot worship before he understands the context of that worship experience. This is our problem. We must speak to man about the God he is seeking with new words and new ways — to give him a basic theology — interesting, well written books — catechetical centers, where not only his mind but his heart can be fed. We must learn to speak honestly and candidly about every issue that concerns man; every sacred premise must be set up, explored and challenged. If these cannot survive examination and challenge, let it be done away with. This is no time for sacred cows.

We are proposing that an experimental center should be established in one of our large cities to explore the basic relationship of life in terms that are meaningful and significant to modern man, which could lead to a redeeming transforming experience. This project could start with selected lay-clergy groups working together. Where conceivable, sufficient dynamics could be generated by the participants so they, in turn, could become leaders of small cells in their own communities. As part of this experimental situation, it is also proposed that a conference on a national level be held for selected clergymen to be trained in these procedures, which, afterwards would become a part of the seminary curriculum.

Mass Media

We live in a new world which is characterized by a return of sorts to the world of "pre-alphabet man." The use of the printed word is now only a limited part of our sensory apparatus, for our senses now are constantly bombarded by an increasing host of multi-images, sound, light feeling, smell. It is significant that the Columbus flood victims chose their television sets as the first object to be saved.

We must develop the awareness that more than anything else in our times, more than the atom, more than the computer—it is the mass media which is changing the face of our world. It has invaded our homes and is part of our most personal experiences, appealing to man at every level of his being. The Christian Church has not yet fully understood the impact of this total upheaval of society and, consequently, has left mass media for the most part, to the secularist who has nothing to express but the barrenness of the contemporary scene, and who is far removed from the norms of human experience and behavior. We now suddenly have become aware that we are at the complete mercy of a handful of media makers who control this vast power. The violence and indecent and obsene elements flowing into our homes and society is the media masters' arbitrary decision and not our choice.

The editorial decisions of a small group of editors and newspaper and magazine owners gives prominence to the acts of lawlessness, thereby inciting an entire chain of reaction undermining law and encouraging anarchy. Recent studies have indicated that hostile tendencies in children have been intensified and aggravated by exposing children to scenes of violence.

It lies with us, as members of the Church and responsible members of American society, to be aware of these forces and to exercise by responsible action, our concern to keep under control obscene, indecent and violent elements in literature, television, radio, and movies. Implied is our cooperation with other churches to advance these ends.

In light of our awareness, we must better use the vast possibilities of mass media to expand our use of multi-images to convey to the total man the timeless dimensions of redemption, for there is much in the secular world that has changed and remedied the ancient maladies of man. The arts must return to their original purpose as the handmaiden of religion to convey eternal truths.

We have a thrilling opportunity to represent to our times the total impact on the whole sensory world of man that lies latent within the aesthetics of the Byzantine Church. It is perhaps here, within the total imaginative life of modern man that his renewal can take place. Not only his mind, but the whole of him must be affected.

We suggest that the next clergy-laity congress be designed as an experiment in multi-media to demonstrate new possibilities. Also we recommend that the Clergy-Laity Album, to be distributed in November, be designed in a manner to convey a living picture of what happened at Athens, 1968.

The Dignity of Man

The chief gift of the Christian community is the concept of uniqueness and precious value of every man. Jesus of Nazareth endows human life with beauty and dignity.

Human rights are the divine birthright of every human being. Because of these, every man must have the opportunity and right of earning a living, of raising his children in decent surroundings, and seeing them obtain the finest education possible. He must be free and encouraged to exercise his responsibilities as a citizen. The degrading and soul-killing qualities of hopeless poverty are stumbling blocks forever to the attainment of the dignity of man.

We stand committed to every cause that genuinely elevates the dignity of man.

Civil Disobedience—The Draft and the Law

We are witnessing in our times, an unparalleled wave of demonstrations, marches, riots, and burning of draft cards, all of which have seen a disturbing ebb of respect for law and even love of country. Violence seems to be the emerging instrument of coercing our private and social goals whether we be individuals, or members of various power blocks.

We recognize the right and obligation to organized and lawful demonstrations, but stand wholly opposed to those who, in the name of some cause, would trespass the rights of others, trample the law underfoot, cause arson, looting, and physical harm to their fellow citizens and who ignore the fact that their rights terminate where the rights of their neighbor begins.

A nation can exist only as long as its citizens uphold its laws and refrain from irresponsible acts. Love of country remains an indispensable ingredient for the survival of our nation. A strong and stable family structure is the greatest safeguard against anarchy and lawlessness. We cannot but deplore those who instruct our young men to evade military service and to destroy their draft cards. The price of freedom has never been free. The privilege of preserving cherished rights and liberties is also the privilege of serving one's nation when those sacred rights are threatened.

Crime

We deplore the continuing increase in crime which in the last seven years has been outdistancing the population by a ratio of almost 9 to 1. The freedom our people have fought and died for is now threatened by anarchy and chaos in the streets. We ask: How free is a nation where a third of its people fear to venture out of their homes and walk their streets after dark?

It is the responsibility of government at all levels to protect its people. We, therefore, ask for strict law enforcement, not only by police but by the courts. We must reestablish the rule of law and respect for law. We must reestablish a system of social self-protection that is clear, definite, and unshakable...one that inspires respect because it works. It means cracking down on those who defy the law, not only from the outside but on officials and judges who weaken and corrupt it from within. It means reasserting authority where authority belongs, instead of artfully remodeling legal concepts to always benefit defendants and never the general public.

We believe that crime will be reduced when the criminal is convinced that if he commits a crime, his apprehension will be swift, his trial prompt, and his sentence substantial.

We reiterate the eloquent expression of Abraham Lincoln: "Let reverence for the laws be breathed by every American mother to the lisping babe that prattles on her lap. Let it be taught in schools, in seminaries, and in colleges. Let it be written in primers, spelling books and in almanacs. Let it be preached from the pulpit, proclaimed in legislative halls and enforced in courts of justice. And in short, let it become the political religion of the nation."

War and Peace

Holy Friday, when the best of us was hung on a cross, comes each springtime to remind us of the continued presence of evil in the world. Until the Kingdom of God finally comes, there will be hate and violence and corruption and exploitation; there will be murder and slavery of every kind. And tragically, there will also be war, which is the most loathsome and the most hideous and demonic form of inhumanity diametrically opposed to everything for which the Christian Church stands. War is hell, but the alternatives are sometimes a nightmare beyond comprehension. We implore our President to keep seeking a solution that is just and equitable, but we stand solidly behind him in his agony to preserve these ideals which comprise the essence of our humanity.

We appeal to Hanoi and Peking and Moscow to take seriously the pursuit of peace and to find the way in Paris to end the holocaust.

War is an ugly thing, but not the ugliest thing. The decayed and degraded state of moral and patriotic feelings, which thinks nothing is worth a war, is worse. A man who has nothing which he cares about more than his personal safety is a miserable creature who has no chance of being free, unless made and kept so by the exertions of better men than himself.

John Stuart Mill

20TH CLERGY-LAITY CONGRESS. 1970, NEW YORK

Social and Moral Issues Committee

A Proposal for the Establishment of an Office of Social Concerns

It is no longer necessary to argue for the need of our Church to speak clearly and act consistently in areas of moral and social concern. Both our history and our theology point to the need for our Church to be involved with both mind and hands in the moral and social issues of our times.

In consequence, there is a definite and clear-cut need for our Church to organize and direct the Orthodox Christian's response to these questions. It is not enough to parcel out the responsibility for this concern in bits and pieces to the Youth Department, the Laity Department, the Philoptochos, the Religious Education Department.

For many years, and during the last three Clergy-Laity Congresses, this need has been evident and on each of these occasions, the Committee on Social and Moral Issues has recommended the establishment of an Office of Social Concerns whose task would be to inform priests and parishes on the Orthodox Church's positions on current issues, set priorities, help parishes and Archdiocesan Districts respond in meaningful ways to the issues of the day in their local areas, assist the parishes to organize local social action committees and provide direction and guidance for them to function, and finally, inform and inspire general action through frequent communication with a newsletter.

Eventually, an Office of Social Concerns on the Archdiocesan District level and in the state, regional and local areas could be implemented.

Ideally, the recommendation of the previous Congresses should be put into practice: that a full-time Office of Social Concerns be established. The most clear and obvious objection to the establishment of this office is the lack of funds. The Committee on Moral and Social Issues feels so strongly that some direction and organization is needed in this area; that if it be necessary, a part-time office should be created immediately to begin meeting the almost chaotic situation which our Church faces in this area.

We strongly recommend that the Congress urge the appointment of at least a part-time director of this office. An interested clergyman with adequate background, or a faculty member of one of the institutions, could perhaps fill this position.

One of the important duties of this office must be the designation of resource people to prepare position papers on current social and moral issues at least six months prior to the Clergy-Laity Congress for use by the Committee on Social and Moral Issues.

This office, of course, would work in close cooperation with His Eminence, the Archdiocese staff and the Bishops of the Archdiocesan districts, as well as the priests and church councils of our parishes.

This committee considers this action item on the agenda as extremely important, not only for our Church as an institution, but also for the spiritual, moral and social well-being of ourselves and our children.

Drug Abuse

The awareness of drug abuse, primarily among the youth of our nation, has caused a great deal of concern to responsible people. The availability of drugs and the call from some for the relaxation of laws concerning the use of drugs has increased the drug flow to alarming proportions.

There has been a tremendous increase in the use of marijuana. Marijuana has often proved to be the introduction to the use of hard drugs.

It is imperative, therefore, that existing laws be maintained and, where needed, strengthened. Law enforcement is not the total, nor the best answer—for addiction and abuse precede arrest. The solution to the problem lies in the beginning of the abuse.

Drug abuse is symptomatic of deeper and more profound problems that affect our society. It must be determined what drives a person to seek out drugs and how these drugs become available. The young people of today must be raised in an environment of Christian love and faith. We urge our parishes to join forces with law enforcement officials and educating bodies to properly instruct our youth. Finally, once addiction has begun, all efforts must be made to seek rehabilitation for those addicted drug abusers, as well as the hard-core addicted.

Race Relations

The Civil Rights Movement of the 1960's brought to the attention of the nation, in dramatic fashion, the many forms of overt and hidden racial discrimination that exist in American society. While all of us have been impoverished spiritually by this stigma upon our nation, minority groups of color such as the Blacks, the American Indians, and the Mexican-Americans have borne the brunt of this malady.

Acutely aware of the racial problems in our nation, Archbishop Iakovos notes in his opening speech to the 20th Clergy-Laity Congress that "our contribution to the abolishment of racial segregation and on behalf of social justice, are of a most imperative nature... our Church...has never restricted its love and philanthropy from those 'outside its fold'." We fully concur with this observation. A divided nation, with entrenched racial hostilities, contradicts the Christian gospel that preaches a oneness and unity among people in which there is neither Jew nor Greek, slave nor free, male nor female.

In recent years, gains have been made in the United States destined to improve race relations, especially in our legislatures and courts. We applaud these gains and call upon all faithful Greek Orthodox Christians to support these achievements morally and in practice. However, we also recognize that there is still much ground to be covered. Housing patterns of discrimination in the Black ghettos and white suburbs still persist in many pockets of the nation. The poverty subsistence of numerous Mexican-American migrant workers is but a product of traditional discriminatory employment practices. The plight of the American Indians on primitive reservations living in abject poverty and hunger, with poor educational opportunities, reflects another tragic result of racial discrimination.

We call upon the Greek Orthodox Christians to use their fullest resources in the struggle for human justice for all people, regardless of race, creed, or color. Specifically, we make these suggestions for social action:

1. That Orthodox Christians become involved in neighborhood organizations which welcome minority people into their neighborhoods and try to promote racial harmony.

2. That Orthodox encourage greater contacts between Orthodox Christians and Christians of other racial groups in an effort to increase better understanding.

3. That Orthodox enter into local projects designed to improve race relations through the tutoring of disadvantaged persons, by helping them help themselves, and through similar programs with like purpose.

4. That Orthodox urge governmental leaders to support legislative measures designed to support and promote racial equality.

We deplore violence as a means of achieving racial harmony and encourage all Greek Orthodox Christians to avoid the extreme groups of both the Right and Left which advocate violent measures.

We believe that in today's affluent and technological society, it is possible to make our world socially hospitable for all men while simultaneously promoting Christ's gospel of spiritual rebirth. Finally, we reaffirm our Church's teaching on the supreme value and worth of every human being in God's sight. Christ died for all men and displayed equal concern for the welfare of every person... beginning in this life and in this world. These are the same ideals we of the Greek Orthodox Church in America aspire to live out in the last third of the 20th century.

Abortion

At the mid-point of the deliberations of the Congress and in this State of New York, the most liberal Abortion Law ever enacted into law in the United States has taken effect. Over 1,000 women wait in line for abortion in the municipal hospitals of this city!

It is incumbent upon us, at this crucial hour to make our witness to the people of this city, the United States and the world and to reinforce the faithful on this most important moral and social issue of our times.

For the Orthodox Church, abortion has been a course of action which is not harmonious with the life in Christ and a rejection of the most elementary and fundamental principles of the Faith.

Throughout the centuries the Orthodox Church has, in its preaching, teaching and canon law, regarded abortion as an evil.

At a time when some states have liberalized abortion laws so radically, it becomes incumbent upon us to speak out. We first must give a clarion call to all the people of our nation warning them of this serious violation of the reverence for life by the indiscriminate exercises of abortion. It is our prophetic responsibility to condemn this law as immoral.

Secondly, we must advise our faithful that no matter what the civil law may permit to the citizens of the nation, the spiritual and moral standards under which we live as Christians and members of the Orthodox Faith prohibit the practice of abortion. We urge our Archdiocese to clarify and disseminate the position of our Church relative to the specific cases and issues which the individual Christian may face regarding the whole issue of abortion.

War and Peace

Peace on earth stands perhaps, as the single, most desired objective of decent good people the world over. Yet it appears that this goal seems more remote and illusive today than at any other time in the history of man. The last fifty years have witnessed the greatest carnage and destruction of human life and the unleashing of demonic forces unparalleled in any other period of man's life on earth.

What we must never for a moment forget, is that those secularist, demonic, anti-human forces, both of the Right and of the Left have in no way been contained.

This Congress goes on record to commend every effort and every movement to terminate war and hostility in every area, whether it be Southeast Asia, the Middle East or anywhere else.

We offer our prayers for our President, that he will find an equitable termination to war. We appeal, as well, once again to Moscow, Hanoi, and Peking to take seriously the pursuit of peace and to find the way in Paris to end the holocaust.

Crime and Punishment

In 1966 and 1968 we stressed the need to curb the spiraling crime rate and the lawlessness that has permeated our society. The picture today is still a dismal one. The staggering statistics are known to all who read the newspapers. We demand that our people receive adequate protection by new legislation and new enforcement support so that we may look forward with hope that future endeavors will strike a fair and stable balance between the power of the state in criminal law and the rights of the individual criminal suspect. We feel our public order is in jeopardy. If that breaks down, freedom will be lost.

We urge our Greek Orthodox communities, usually identified as having strong family ties, to be aware of the attacks on our Christian values. We urge our communicants to strengthen family ties, to be patient, understanding, and receptive to the questions and aspirations of our youth and our aged.

Finally, we call upon all communicants, of every age, to respect the right of peaceful assembly and the expression of opinion, which is the essence of the freedom we enjoy by virtue of the sacrifices of our maternal and paternal forefathers.

Pornography

We deplore the increase in the spread of pornography in America, and we urge that our Church in all levels expand its participation in the various movements and commissions to eliminate pornography.

Ecology

The young people of this nation have been largely instrumental recently in bringing to our attention the developing crisis with regard to our environment and man's defilement of the Lord's creation. Man's tremendous technological and scientific advances must be seen as achievement of his creative calling under God. This does not, however, justify the brutalization and wanton destruction of our environment which was perpetrated in the name of scientific development. We are reminded that we have a paramount responsibility to the whole of creation. We call upon the citizens of this land and of the world to harness their intellects and energies to reduce to the absolute minimum the defilement of our environment and the destruction of the balance of nature whatever sacrifice in comfort and money may be involved.

21ST CLERGY-LAITY CONGRESS. 1972, HOUSTON, TEXAS

Social and Moral Issues Committee

Measures for the Development
of an Orthodox Christian Social Conscience

The Social and Moral Issues Committee met in order to review the accomplishments of the past and in order to define the task of the Greek Orthodox Archdiocese for the ensuing two years in this area. Three fundamental affirmations were made by the Committee:

1. That the thrice-repeated Congress request recommendation in Montreal, Athens, and New York (1966-1968-1970) calling for the establishment of an office of Social Concerns to be established

now with a full time director at Archdiocesan Headquarters in order to organize, implement, and develop a coordinated program of education and action in the area of social concern. Toward this purpose the Moral and Social Issues Committee has made appropriate recommendation to the Finance Committee.

2. That there is need to raise the consciousness of our people regarding the implications of our Orthodox Christian faith for the social issues of our time. It is time for the Orthodox Christians of America to challenge themselves and the people of our nation with the affirmation that Christ is Lord of all the world and that He is the answer to the problems of every society.

3. That we speak concretely at this Congress to the social implications of the Orthodox Christian teaching for our own community life and for some of the serious issues of our day.

Social and Moral Issues in the Life of the Parish

The Church as the "Leaven" of Society

The Congress recognizes the fact that the Church has always served as the "leaven" of society. In their own way, the Greek Orthodox churches in the Americas have performed a significant role and contributed to the life and progress of the society in which we live simply by being what it is—the Church of God here in this place and at this time. The good influence of the Orthodox Church on the faithful, both young and old, has been and continues to be an outgrowth of the Church's effort to be true to herself. The Church is proud of its members of all social, educational and public positions, who have been continuing forces for good in our society. In this, the Church has served as a "leaven" which has made the world more pleasing to God. This Congress, however, also recognizes that our organized parish life does not always embody to the fullest extent possible this responsibility to be the "leaven" of our society.

The Integrity of Church Message and Parish Practice

The Congress notes that the witness of the believing community is often marred by the agreement between the ideals and faith which we preach and the practice of them in our own organized life. Often, what is said from the pulpit, Gospel lectern, and Church School podium is ignored and contradicted in the most flagrant of ways in the decisions of our councils, committees and groups. Because this is not always a conscious contradiction, but usually reflects our failure as a Christian people to consciously seek to make our fund-raising and administrative decisions in the light of our faith, this Congress feels that it is necessary to alert the members of our parishes to the need for the integrity of the Church's moral and spiritual message and our parish practices, especially those which deal with fundraising.

The Orthodox Christian Faith and Certain Fundraising Methods

This Congress is fully aware of the struggle on the part of leaders, both clergy and lay, to raise the funds for the various programs of the Church, both local and national. It is an important and difficult task. Often, the pressures of fundraising lead us to the decision to use methods which are inappropriate to our calling to serve God in our Christian community. The Congress is alarmed to note the increasing use of fundraising methods in our parishes which are not in harmony with the moral and spiritual traditions of our Holy Orthodox faith. More and more parishes are accepting the "easy" income from activities such as Bingo, Las Vegas Nights, Fortune Telling, the rental of parish facilities for commercial gambling enterprises, as well as the deceptive transfer of gambling activities for the benefit of the parish to "neutral" places under the direction of so-called "non-church" agencies. Orthodox Christians should be fully aware of the destructive consequences of these practices upon our own integrity and the influence that it has upon our society and our own people. There is need to develop a strong sense of Christian stewardship to counteract these fundraising methods.

Making Decisions for Parish Life

Of primary concern to this Congress is that all our communities begin to relate their social and fundraising programs to the central spiritual and moral message of our Orthodox Christian faith. As questions of decisions arise in our councils and committees, and as these actions are discussed and decided upon, it is imperative for our parish leaders, both clergy and lay, to submit every proposal to the measure of Christ. It is inconceivable to this Congress, for example, how church councils can continue to divorce their fundraising efforts from the most simple considerations of Christian ethics. The mental and spiritual gymnastics which permit some church councils to raise money for the Church, for example, through the presentation of "oriental dancers" as entertainment at parish functions must end. Such decision-making does no honor to the leaders; it expresses failure to comprehend the message of the Church; it disgusts the youth of our time which seeks honesty and integrity on the part of church leadership; and it presents to the world a hypocritical church life. Those entrusted with making decisions for every aspect of the life of the parish owe it to the heritage of the faith, to the faithful membership and to the society in which we live, to make every decision in the spirit of Christ and His Holy Church. Faith and action should not be separate. There is a dramatic need for consistency in pronouncement and deed in our fundraising efforts. This Congress challenges our prishes to make that need a reality.

The Task of Our Parishes in the Coming Years

The parish is not primarily a fundraising institution. It raises funds in order to do its work. This Clergy-Laity Congress would call every parish of the Archdiocese to reexamine its understanding of its work. For many of our church communities, concern for the erection of new buildings has held the center stage of concern. It appears that for most of our parishes, this task of building churches and educational centers has been most beautifully and adequately realized. Is it not our task now to redirect our energies and resources to programs which will translate our faith into action? This Congress urges every parish in the Archdiocese to seriously reassess its understanding of its work; to ask whether it is not time now to spend our funds, time and talents for the building up of the human material before us; to plan to use our resources most effectively for the spiritual and moral regeneration of our own people and society at large. Here, the leadership of the priest is crucial. He must not only be the example of the Christian faith and life for the faithful. There is an urgent demand that he communicate vitally these new priorities to the faithful. The new orientation of parish life from brick and mortar to spirit, life and behavior needs to be embodied in every level of our organized church life. We would strongly urge the *Orthodox Observer*, our youth and Religious Education Department to embody this direction in all of their efforts.

Individual Employment and Our Identity as Orthodox Christians

What is asked of parishes is also asked of us as individuals. As Orthodox Christians, we are employed in many occupations, businesses, professions, and jobs through which we earn our livelihood. This Congress challenges every Orthodox Christian to examine himself and to ask if there is a fundamental harmony between his faith and his work. Integrity is needed here also. The choice of our work; how it influences the world about us; how it expresses our commitment to Christ and His Church; the opportunities it provides us with to work for a more Christlike society, are questions which each individual Greek Orthodox Christian must ask of himself. Sincere faith will lead some of us to recognize that our daily work can be harmonized with our Orthodox Christian commitment. Others of us will see new ways to change our work patterns so that the spiritual and ethical dimensions and opportunities of our employment can be enhanced. Many of us will see how our Christian witness can be embodied and made more clear and strong through our work. The message of Astonaut James Irwin to this Congress is a perfect example which this Congress commmends to all of our Orthodox faithful. Those in the professions are especially charged with this responsibility. The physician, attorney, journalist, educator, communications specialist, consultant, and elected official must never forget that they are first of all sons and daughters of God, servants of the Lord Jesus Christ and responsible members of His Holy Orthodox Church. Above all, the clergyman must never forget the requirement that he is to be, in both work and deed, the examplar for the faithful.

Organizing for Effective Diaconia

There is need to organize ourselves for more effective work on the part of the Church in terms of the vital moral and spiritual issues which will increasingly face us as individuals, as parishes, as Archdiocesan districts and as an Archdiocese. Toward this purpose, this Congress not only approves the establishment and funding of an Archdiocesan Office of Social and Moral Concerns, but also recommends that each Archdiocesan District Clergy-Laity Council establish a "Social and Moral Concerns" Committee to coordinate district efforts in this area. In addition, this Congress urges parish priests, church councils, and parish general assemblies, to establish local parish committees on "Social and Moral Concerns." Guidelines for such committees should be provided by the Archdiocesan Office.

Facing the Social Issues of the World

The Clergy-Laity Congress, in addition to concerning itself with the Orthodox Christian community, finds it of equal necessity to turn to the society and world in which we live with an Orthodox Christian witness. We review with great alarm numerous trends in our society which indicate a social and moral deterioration of serious dimensions. We hold that our contemporary society of affluence, technology, pluralism and individual freedom poses both great perils and challenges to the future of our country. But we are equally firm in our conviction that the solution to these many pressing social and moral problems can be found by infusing our spirits with the love of Christ and a firm commitment to His precepts and practices. With this conviction in mind, we undertake to speak to our society at large, to our fellow Christians and to all men and women of good will on these issues. Of the many serious problems which our society faces during these critical days, we have selected only a few for special comment. Without minimizing the importance of any of the major issues which we as a people face, this Congress has chosen to speak on the topics of drug abuse, race relations, the family in contemporary society, law, order and justice, and the topic of war and peace. To these burning issues of the times we would also speak.

Drug Abuse

The development in recent years of what has been described as the "drug culture" has justifiably caused great concern among all responsible elements of our society. We strongly share this concern; in particular, as it affects our youth, and would point out that the problem of drug abuse is now beginning to reach our young people, who we previously thought might escape the ravages of this terrible scourge.

We realize that law enforcement agencies and other institutions have started to mount large-scale education, information and prevention programs aimed at warning young people in public schools about the dangers of drug abuse. Despite these many programs, we believe it incumbent on the Archdiocese and its communities to initiate immediately programs aimed at combatting the drug problem because we believe it necessary that our young people receive the Christian reasons for avoiding this blight.

To reach both parents and youth about this problem, we suggest the following proposals be adopted:

1. That extensive articles or supplements be printed in the *Orthodox Observer*, in Greek and English, providing basic information on drug abuse to parents. It is important that this information be presented simply and clearly. The material should instruct parents on how to detect if their children are on drugs; how they might prevent children from using drugs, and how to react if they have youngsters using drugs. Above all, it should urge parents to educate themselves on the recognition, use and dangers of drugs.

2. Each community should establish a drug education program,

either by creating its own committee on drug abuse or arranging for outside speakers, or experts to lecture children and parents about the drug problems.

3. If feasible, every Diocese should organize a drug abuse committee to assist local parishes in creating drug abuse programs and tie in the local parish work with activities at the Archdiocesan level. We would point out and commend the Archdiocesan Office of Youth Affairs for already circulating to the communities some well prepared information booklets on drug abuse.

In making the above recommendations, we fully realize that many priests and local communities have achieved notable results in drug education projects, and we sincerely hope that the other communites will initiate their example. On the other hand, the Committee holds that the ultimate answer to avoiding such soul-destroying practices as drug abuse, is to embrace the Gospel and teachings of Christ.

Race Relations

Our contribution to the abolishment of racial segregation and on behalf of social justice, is of a most imperative nature. We heartily reaffirm this age-old position of the Orthodox Church. We call upon all Greek Orthodox Christians to devote themselves to the task of eliminating racial discrimination from our society, in all its insidious forms.

Social movements of recent years indicate that Americans of goodwill are ready and eager to support efforts which will assure equal education, equal employment, open housing and equal opportunities for human development for people who have been denied them in the past. The conscience of America can no longer tolerate injustices registered against others simply because their skin pigmentation happens to be something other than white. Racial hatred and prejudice, expressed most overtly in the past against the American Indians, the Blacks and the Chicanos contradicts the Christian Gospel of love which proclaims that in Jesus Christ there is neither Jew nor Greek, slave nor free, male nor female.

We applaud the gains achieved in race relations in recent years and call upon all Orthodox Christians to support them both morally and in practice. We acknowledge that the battle to conquer racial discrimination on a national scale, through changed attitudes and concrete social action, has just begun. It must continue. Specific problems needful of our attention, prayers, and actions are:

1. American Indians still living at a poverty level on reservations that offer little or no opportunities for an improved life.

2. Black Americans still oppressed by a high degree of unemployment and underemployment, ghetto housing, and inferior education.

3. Brown Americans who frequently receive starvation wages for hard and long physical labor (for example, migrantworkers), and who are still subjected to the same patterns of discrimination perpetuated for so long against Blacks.

We recommend the folling course of action by Greek Orthodox Christians to correct these wrongs:

1. Promote local study and action groups in the parish that will foster maximum understanding among different races. In other words, cultivating Christ-centered hearts.

2. Contacting and encouraging government officials at all levels to support and enforce measures of legislation that guarantee equal opportunities to every American, regardless of color. In other words, creating a Christian system of just laws.

These two ideals, the sensitive heart and the just law, spring out of our Orthodox Christian heritage. They can in practice, make America a hospitable society for all people, despite the accident of color which God has given them.

We pledge ourselves, as Greek Orthodox Christians trying to live in obedience to the Gospel of love, to pray and work for racial harmony, understanding and equal treatment in every dimension of living. The time for racial discrimination has ended. The time for brotherhood has come.

The Family in Contemporary Society

As we approach matters of social and moral concern, our thoughts turn to the original Holy Creation according to the Holy Scripture that God created man in His image and likeness (Genesis). One of the most vital and extremely critical problems that disturbs our modern society, and which concerns each one of us personally, is the moral decline and importance of the Christian family. We believe that the family's declining influence is a major factor behind much of our society's current malaise.

With this in mind, the Social and Moral Issues Committee views with great alarm current trends of social and moral deterioration which are contrary to Christian ethics and practice. Among the more disturbing elements of this trend are: the breakdown of traditional family relationships; the confusion over the social and moral roles of male and female; the increase in crime and acts of violence; the strong pressure for abortions, and the increasing prevalence in the mass media of pornographic and other salacious materials which seek to exploit man's weaknesses rather than elevate his sights to new spiritual and philanthropic levels.

Obviously, the answers to many of these problems rest with the home where the parents must assume chief responsibility for imparting the fundamentals of Christian ethics, behavior and stewardship. At the same time, however, the Church and the communicants must confront responsible changes in society, life-styles, economic practices and many other aspects which heretofore have been considered as immutable and timeless.

Another social plague of our times is the perversions of "the natural use," "of men and women," into that which is against nature (Rom. 1.26), the condition of lesbians and homosexuals (Rom. 1. 27). Unfortunately, for this great country, although against God's commandments and our Lord's teachings, it is being discussed to become legally permissible, and organized into religious cults. A further social problem is that of venereal disease. The increase of sexual promiscuity has reached epidemic proportions. We reaffirm that the basic solution is the restoration of the Christian view of the sacred and proper respect for premarital sexual purity.

"Speaking the truth in love" (Eph. 4.15), "for it is shame even to speak of those things which are done of them in secret" (Eph. 5.12), our Church must take strict measures to bring the mother as co-creater and as a wife to her spiritual kingdom—the Christian family, offering love to her husband and family.

This is the responsibility of the Church. The Church through the servants of God and particularly the members of the clergy must work to rededicate ourselves to save the Christian family by teaching and "speaking the truth in love"; by sermons; in Bible classes; by Catechisms; by reestablishing the sacramental life, especially Repentance; Holy Confession and Holy Communion; and by becoming a living example of the Orthodox faith and practice and, according to our Lord, by becoming "the light of the world" and "the salt of the earth," that is, "becoming all things to all men that we may save all, " according to the eternal word of God.

We must also take note of a number of rather pernicious philosophies and pseudo-philosophical fads which in recent years have attracted many unsuspecting adherents and, in particular, the young, who are seeking new meanings and experiences. Some of the more prominent of these un-Christian ideologies are witchcraft, astrology, occult forms, and other so-called exotic religions which promote superstition and anti-Christian attitudes.

These manifestations of human instability and sinfulness reflect, in this Committee's view, that modern man is in great need of re-establishing his relationship with Jesus Christ. It is, therefore, to this great mission which the Church must now direct her full attention. Every hierarch, clergyman and communicant should be involved in trying to permeate the family, our institutions, social and fraternal organizations, with a sound Christian spirit so vital for meeting the challenge posed by modern society.

Our Greek Orthodox communities are usually identified as having strong family ties. We urge our communicants to strengthen those family ties, to be patient and compassionate, and receptive to the yearnings and aspirations of our youth and aged. We urge our parishes to constantly seek the truth in love and to be eternally vigilant against the attacks on our Christian values.

Law and Order with Justice

Crime rates are increasing thoughout our nation and lawlessness not only permeates our society but also subverts social stability.

We, therefore, demand that all segments of our society be protected with vigorous law-and-order enforcement support on all levels of govenment. We commend the organization of federal, state, regional, and local crime strike forces, especially against pushers, as a necessary multitudinous approach and ultimate solution to the problems of crime. We also commend constructive court reform procedures wherever undertaken in order to break the log-jam of backlogged court cases and to process reasonably and expeditously the prosecution of those arrested.

We are, however, also mindful that law and order must be tempered with justice and consequently all our endeavors must strike a fair and stable balance between the power of the state in criminal law and rights of the individual criminal suspect.

Furthermore, we urge that the Congress of the United States enact adequate and reasonable gun control legislation so that the unauthorized and improper use of guns may be thwarted.

In the area of prison reform the committee would urge this Congress to exercise a greater awarness of the correctional injustice that exists in our society; the need to improve prison facilities, antiquated and overcrowded in most states, to provide appropriate rehabilitation and training programs for inmates, and to urge a general updating of the entire penal system aimed at treating the detained offender humanely.

We believe that freedom, order, and justice are indivisible and inseparate. In our society today, law and order with justice should be emphasized, for without order freedom is meaningless and without freedom, justice becomes nonexistent.

And ultimately, perennially, and from all ages, can there be any real freedom, any real order in society and real justice, without the redeeming force and power of our Lord Jesus Christ? We can only be really free if we seek the truth in Jesus, whose blood was shed for our redemption. And how can there be justice without love, for God so loved the world that He gave His only begotten Son for our salvation.

The Lord Jesus Christ is the only present and ultimate answer!

Peace

A concern of top priority to this Congress is the establishment of peace in Vietnam. We appeal to all people of goodwill, especially to those committed to the teachings of Christ, to pray and work for peace in this devastated nation.

The wars of the 20th century, history's most destructive, affirm that war destroys, kills, wastes, and embitters. It provides no cures. It produces no victors. Vietnam offers latest testimony to these tragic facts. Already too many have died and suffered. Too much has been wasted. Too often we have heard false reports of a termination.

We urge ceaseless activity towards the goal of peace in Vietnam, especially by the leaders of all nations involved on both sides. Also, we appeal to all world leaders to work towards this end.

We who have been called the "sons of God" when we pursue the avenues that make peace, pledge ourselves to labor in all possible ways to bring peace in Vietnam. No time can be too soon for the conclusion of this tragic war.

22ND CLERGY-LAITY CONGRESS, 1974, CHICAGO
Social and Moral Issues Committee

Measures for the Development of an
Orthodox Christian Social Conscience

In line with the Archbishop's keynote address and the theme of Congress the Social and Moral Issues Committee met in order to review the accomplishments of the past and in order to define the task of the Greek Orthodox Archdiocese for the ensuing two years in this area. Three fundamental affirmations were made by the Committee.

1. That the often repeated Congress request recommendation in Montreal, Athens, New York, and Houston calling for the establishment of an Office of Social Concerns to be established now with a full-time director at the Archdiocesan Headquarters in order to organize, implement and develop a coordinated program of education and action in areas of social concerns. Towards this purpose the Moral and Social Issues Committee has made appropriate recommendation to the Finance Committee in the amount of forty thousand dollars annually.

2. That there is need to raise the consciousness of our people regarding the implications of our Orthodox Christian faith for the social issues of our time. It is time for the Orthodox Christians of America to challenge themselves and the people of our nation with the affirmation that Christ is Lord of all the world and that He is the answer to the problems of every society.

3. That we speak concretely at this Congress to the social implications of Orthodox Christians teaching for our own community and for some of the serious issues of our day.

Social and Moral Issues in the Life of the Parish
The Church as the 'Leaven' of Society

The Congress recognizes the fact that the Church has always served as the 'leaven' of society. In their own way, the Greek Orthodox churches in the Americas have performed a significant role and contributed to the life and progress of the society in which we live, simply by being what it is—the Church of God here in this place and at this time. The good influence of the Orthodox Church on the faithful, both young and old, had been and continues to be an outgrowth of the Church's effort to be true to herself. The Church is proud of its members of all social, educational and public positions who have been continuing forces for good in our society. In this, the Church has served as 'leaven' which has made the world more pleasing to God. This Congress, however, also recognizes that our organized parish life does not always embody to the fullest extent possible this responsibility to be the 'leaven' of our society.

It was apparent from the discussion during the meeting of the committee that the moral and social issues of our time demand responsive attention that must come from an informed and responsible source.

In line with this thinking the Committee adopted the following resolution:

1. That a full-time Office of Social Concerns be established now, with a full-time director at the Archdiocesan headquarters, in order to organize, implement and develop a coordinated program of education and action in the area of the social concerns.

2. That a select group of qualified persons be commissioned by the Archdiocese to prepare position papers, presenting the Greek Orthodox position on social and moral issues, updating some when necessary. Distribution to the parishes and mass media should commence immediately after preparation of such papers. Suggested subjects of such position papers should be in addition to others.

1. The Moral Crisis in the Nation.
2. Euthanasia.
3. War/Peace.
4. Evolution.
5. The Right to Life/Abortion.
6. Contraception and Sterilization.
7. Aid to parochial schools
8. Drug Abuse.
9. The Family/Divorce/Mixed Marriages.
10. Venereal Diseases.
11. Gambling/Fundraising.
12. Alcoholism.
13. Capital Punishment.
14. Penal Reform.
15. Equal Opportunity for Human Development.
    a. Minority groups
    b. Women
    c. Busing
    d. Newly arrived immigrants
    e. Senior citizens
16. Freedom of the Press.
17. Religious Liberty.
18. Pornography.
19. Secularization of Society.
20. Amnesty.
21. The Church and Its Relation to Civil Authority.
22. The Church and Social Activism.

23. Homosexuality.
24. Prostitution.
25. Multiculturalism and Multilingualism.

The Integrity of Church Message and Parish Practice

The Congress notes that the witness of the believing community is often marred by the lack of agreement between the ideals and faith which we preach and the practice of our own organized life. Often, what is said from the pulpit, the Gospel lecturn and the Church school podium, is ignored and contradicted in the most flagrant of ways in the decisions of our councils, committees and groups. Because this is not always a conscious contradiction, but usually reflects our failure as a Christian people to consciously seek to make our fundraising and administrative decisions in the light of our faith, this Congress feels that is is necessary to alert the members of our parishes to the need for the integrity of the Church's moral and spiritual message and our parish practices, especially those which deal with fundraising.

The Orthodox Christian Faith and Fundraising Methods

This Congress is fully aware of the struggle on the part of parish leaders, both clergy and lay, to raise the funds for the various programs of the Church, both local and national. It is an important and difficult task. Often, the pressures of fundraising lead us to the decision to use methods which are inappropriate to our calling to serve God in our Christian community. The Congress is alarmed to note the inceasing use of fundraising methods in our parishes which are not in harmony with the moral and spiritual traditions of our Holy Orthodox faith. Orthodox Christians should be fully aware of the destructive consequences of these practices upon our own people. There is need to develop a strong sense of Christian stewardship for the proper raising of funds to sustain and promote community programs.

The Committee felt strongly that gambling in all forms, in connection with fundraising should be forbidden, and that our community fundraising be done looking to other and more respected sources based on Christian stewardship.

Conclusion

The Committee felt that it should be empowered to continue in existence in order to secure implementation of the foregoing recommendations as adopted, thus permitting a standing committee to exist in this sphere of Orthodox life which would help make this work a reality.

Amendment on Abortion

Resolved:

"This Congress reaffirms the teachings of the Church on abortion, and reminds the faithful that abortion on demand, and as a means to population control, is, and has always been, a grave sin. The faithful are, of course, free as individual citizens to promote efforts in the civil sphere to restrict abortion on demand by statute."

23RD CLERGY-LAITY CONGRESS.1976, PHILADELPHIA

Social and Moral Issues Committee Report

The Committee on Social Concerns met under the able chairmanship of His Grace Bishop Gerasimos of Abydos. In the course of its deliberations over the past two days, with the invaluable guidance and patience of the Rev. Dr. Nicon D. Patrinacos, it reviewed and considered in depth drafts of position papers submitted by the Department of Interchurch Relations and Social Concerns on the following vital contemporary topics:

Abortion
Birth Control
Drinking-Alcoholism
Homosexuality
The Danger of Community-overexpansion

These papers were the product of the deliberations of qualified people assigned to this task in accordance with the recommendation of the 22nd Congress. Position papers on other timely social and moral issues will be prepared by the Department of Interchurch Relations and Social Concerns for future dissemination.

The statements as finally refined and developed by the Committee from the drafts submitted to it, and which are presented to this Congress, are for the purpose of providing guidelines for our communicants. These should not be taken as being in the nature of theological pronouncements. Although the ideas and guidelines presented are in accordance with Orthodox theology and tradition, technicalities have been purposely avoided. In this way, the Orthodox Christians will have the benefit of the guidance of his Church for application in his personal life without the hindrance of the complexity of theological statements.

Abortion

The Orthodox Church has a definite, formal and expressed attitude toward abortion.

It condemns all positive procedures purporting to abort the embryo or fetus, whether by surgical or by chemical means.

The Orthodox Church brands abortion as murder; that is, as a premeditated termination of the life of a human being.

Doubts as to when life can be called human in the womb have been dispelled by very recent genetic studies.

According to the findings of these studies, all the characteristics of the human individual, as we know it, are present in the embryo as soon as the process of conception is completed.

These studies indicate that hereditary and personality traits, by which the new individual will be known, are not added or developed gradually as was believed before.

Thus, it makes no difference whether abortion is performed after the determination of pregnancy or later on. In both cases, a human individual is aborted.

This is the reason for which, in the eyes of God and the Church, abortion is tantamount to taking a life.

The only time the Orthodox Church will reluctantly acquiesce to abortion is when the preponderance of medical opinion determines that unless the embryo or fetus is aborted, the mother will die.

Decisions of the Supreme Court and State legislatures, by which abortion with or without restrictions is allowed, should be viewed by practicing Christians as an affront to their beliefs in the sanctity of life.

Birth Control (Prevention of Pregnancy)

The Orthodox Church has no formally expressed position on birth control either for or against it.

However, a number of Fathers and theologians have urged people to avoid interfering with the process of reproduction, thus exercising control over the number of their offspring.

The rationale behind this prohibition relates to the fact that procreation in nature, as well as in one's family, is God's law and will, and as such, cannot be violated for any reason whatsoever.

With regard to human procreation in particular, the belief that God provides personally and individually for all his creatures, excludes any possibility of parental control over the number of their children.

Contemporary concepts of parenthood tend, however, to stress the inescapable responsibilities of husband and wife toward children. These responsibilities have been well defined and are taken to be commensurate with the parents' ability to provide the material and spiritual opportunities that help their children to develop into God-pleasing individuals.

Since parental dynamics and possibilities can be reasonably measureed before pregnancy, today conscientious parents may resort to birth control processes to prevent the unlimited growth to their family. This way they wish to provide adequately for the spiritual upbringing of their offspring as well as their material needs.

The sacrament of matrimony implies a Christian family. Therefore, the Orthodox Church condemns persons who for selfish reasons refuse to have children or limit their number disproportionately to their material and spiritual means and capabilites.

Currents of thought in today's Orthodox Church seem to make no distinction between various means by which birth control can be exercised. Whether by mechanical-chemical means or by abstinence from intercourse, the outcome is prevention of pregnancy. Thus, a moral distinction between the above two ways appears to lack moral content.

The abstinence theory has originated from a theory of sex by which marital intercourse without pregnancy is deemed immoral. However, the Orthodox concept of the Christian marriage does not limit itself to procreation. In addition to this sacred end of marriage, husband and wife in an Orthodox marriage seek also to further develop and possibly perfect their two personalities in the union of marriage. Thus, marital relations that help the sacred purpose of advancing their personalities closer to the reality of true happiness and blessedness under God can hardly be denied to them.

Drinking—Alcoholism

The Orthodox Church condemns habitual drinking that unavoidably leads to alcoholism.

Parents who drink on any pretext whatsoever should always keep in mind that children do not attempt to find excuses for their parents' drinking, but simply follow their example as soon as they themselves are faced with difficulties and look for an escape.

The pressures of social life and personal difficulties do not become lighter by drinking. Drinking is not an escape but a stepping out of harsh reality and into the vacuum of chemical elation. The return becomes more and more painful until one no longer wishes to return to reality.

Drinking parents, even though they may not care for themselves, should realize what drinking can do to the mental, physical, psychological, and spiritual consitution of their children.

They must fully realize that the weaker from among their children, and often the most loving ones, are susceptible to following their example and can be punished with alcoholism as a price for their misfortune of being children of drinking parents.

No parental shortcoming has been copied by children more frequently than that of drinking.

Habitual drinking leading to alcoholism is at the present time assuming dangerous proportions and threatens with destruction not only families but our society as a whole.

In realizing this, the Orthodox Church calls upon parents who use alcohol in order to camouflage their problems to come to the realization of the dangerous situations to which they lead their children and themselves by habitual drinking.

The solution to our difficulties and problems cannot be found in temporary absence from reality by intoxicating ourselves. It is to be found only in a new viewing and approach of experience by way of reclaiming our divine sonship.

Far from stigmatizing the alcoholic, the Orthodox Church has from ancient times dealt with alcoholism as a disease. At the same time, she has warned and condemned those who, for personal or social reasons, drink habitually.

Thus, the Church wishes to state categorically that apart from the few cases of alcoholism, which may be connected to hereditary factors or psychopathological causes, social drinking that becomes a life routine protrays a disturbed individual. A true Christian should seek his therapy by fully assuming rather than avoiding his responsibilities. The only way to restore oneself to the status of his divine sonship is to mend his ways and thereby effectively deal with the causes of his difficulties.

Together with the help available from therapeutic sciences, one should return inwardly to the source of real and lasting power, which is God's love for man.

The Orthodox Church on Homosexuality

The position of the Orthodox Church toward homosexuality has been expressed by synodicals, canons and Patristic pronouncements beginning with the very first centuries of Orthodox ecclesiastical life.

Thus, the Orthodox Church condemns unreservedly all expressions of personal sexual experience which prove contrary to the definite and unalterable function ascribed to sex by God's ordinance and expressed in man's experience as a law of nature.

Thus, the function of the sexual organs of a man and a woman and their biochemical generating forces in glands and glandular secretions are ordained by nature to serve one particular purpose, the procreation of the human kind.

However, the human sexual apparatus appears to have been designed not only as the medium by which the necessary physical contact for the purpose of sex is effected, but as the generator as well and the center of a highly complex system of feelings which all together are known by the name eros, love between husband and wife.

Therefore, any and all uses, of the human sex organs for purposes other than those ordained by creation, runs contrary to the nature of things as decreed by God and produces the following wrongs:

a. They violate God's ordinance regarding both the procreation of man and his emotional life generated by his instinctive attraction to the opposite sex not only for procreating but for advancing the personalities of a man and a woman to a state of completion within the association of the sacrament of marriage. For all this, homosexuality is an insult to God, and since it attempts to alter the laws regulating creation, it is a blasphemy.

b. Homosexuality interferes with the normal development of societal patterns and as such it proves detrimental to all. These endangered patterns include personal values regarding sex which people normally take to be a vital part of their existence and a valuable asset to their living a normal life esteemed by others.

c. The homosexual degrades his own sex and thus denies to himself the self-respect that is generated from the feeling that one is in line with God's creation.

Homosexuality appears to be of two kinds: physico-genetic and habitual. Physico-genetic homosexuality is of physical origin due to secretory abnormalities that may produce organic changes. This type of homosexuality is rather rare and is treated as any other medical disorder.

Habitual homosexuality develops within the waking experience of the sufferer and in full knowledge by him of the changes that take place in his emotional orientation and his general attitude toward life.

Habitual homosexuality may have more than one cause. All, however, point out to a moral failure at some stage of the individual's development, or to the animate environment from which the homosexual originated.

Thus, although homosexuality, followed as a way of life by the sufferer, may be subject to psychopathological investigation and treatment, the origin of it, in all but the few physico-genetic cases mentioned above, brings with it a moral failure. It is because of the realization of this that homosexuality has been described from ancient times as a moral stigma.

Thus, the Orthodox Church cannot subscribe to the demand that homosexuals be recognized by society and its agencies as legal spouses and as deserving the same respect as men and women enjoy in the state of wedlock.

Society and its values, religious and societal, have legitimate claims over the behavior of its members, especially in so vital a function as the sexual one. No one has the right to do whatever he wishes with his body and still claim recognition and respect on the part of society.

The Orthodox Church believes that homosexuality should be treated by society as an immoral and dangerous perversion and by religion as a sinful failure. In both cases, correction is called for. Homosexuals should be accorded the confidential medical and psychiatric facilities by which they can be helped to restore themselves to self-respecting sexual identity that belongs to them by God's ordinance.

In full confidentiality, the Orthodox Church cares and provides pastorally for homosexuals in the belief that no sinner who has failed himself and God should be allowed to deteriorate morally and spiritually.

Psychiatric restoration, without religious direction and reconciliation with God is bound to prove short-lived.

A healthy society and its various religions do not recognize perversions. Rather, they work to restore the homosexual to the status of a self-esteemed individual and thus, to a valued instrument of their own survival and well-being under God.

The Dangers of Community Over-expansion

Religious communities, the goals of which are spiritual by definition, may and are expected to provide themselves with the best of physical facilities, from their place of worship to community halls, and to take pride in achievements of this material nature.

The Greek Orthodox community is not any different; if anything, the love for form of the Greek Orthodox, directly inherited from those who built a Parthenon, appears to generate a deeper psychic need, and as a result, often tends to become the driving force in a given community.

However, the overemphasizing of building and decorating projects in a community, and consequently of mobilizing its entire material forces and manpower, may result in the neglect of the main purpose for which a community is established and functions: the spiritual advancement and personal religious sanctification of its members.

A Greek Orthodox community is as vital and durable as its spiritual force, from the priest to the last churchgoer whose financial capabilities may be small, but whose faith and heart may be great. This type of foundation is the only one that can guarantee the health and long life of the community. If this type of community strength is lacking, the wealth of the richer membership, who can contribute effectively to physical expansion, can help the community little if at all.

Usually, expansion projects that are really needed are sucessfully pursued because they prove to be within the perimeter of the spiritual and material strength of the community.

In many cases, though, expansion programs surpass the limits of all that a community can bear in the nature of mortgages and maintenance obligations.

The reason for this type of over-expansion can be most often traced to a spiritual failure in the community. This failure may be tied with a group spirit seeking consciously or subconsciously, communal pride in an attempt to convince others and the community members themselves of how good and able they really are.

Or, it may simply be symptomatic of little or no spiritual life in the community and thus it may constitute a camouflaged attempt at diverting the eyes of the community from its spiritual deprivation to the escape of feeling self-fulfilled in the magnificence of a beautiful house of worship and other community buildings. People usually forget that a spiritually insensitive congregation does not become any more spiritual in a beautiful church, even if psychologically they may feel more pleased with themselves. Actually, they may be led to believe that their beautiful surroundings for worship have made them more beautiful in reflection. Although this feeling is real, it is unfortunately a fleeting one, lasting only for as long as one is in artistically imposing surroundings.

Still more, there are instances in which communities embark on over-expanding projects without full consideration of the spiritual and financial strength of the congregation. But as soon as it becomes apparent that the expansion, in spite of the new facilities it has provided and the community pride it has generated, has been overly ambitious, it brings about estrangements, withdrawls, and even community polarization.

In conformity with the adage, "poverty breeds dissension," an over-expanded community will continue to pay the penalties of a spiritual failure of this kind for a long time. Actually, a community which embarks on a miscalculated physical expansion would have reached its goals sooner had it proceeded in line and in conformity with its inner spiritual forces, which alone should dictate its program of expansion.

No beautiful churches and no imposing community buildings can balance the loss of love in a community.

What would a Greek Orthodox community profit if it "won the whole world, but lost its soul?"

24TH CLERGY-LAITY CONGRESS. 1978, DETROIT

Social and Moral Issues Committee

The Social and Moral Concerns Committee of the 24th Clergy-Laity Congress limited itself to request the Archdiocese to study fifteen issues of social concern taken primarily from the area of bioethics. These topics are:

1. Divorce
2. Interfaith marriage
3. Child abuse
4. Pornography
5. Human rights
6. Equal rights
7. Euthanasia, death and dying (life support systems)
8. Donation of organs after death.
9. Arms race (disarmament)
10. Cremation
11. Criminal justice
12. Abortion
13. Embryo fertilization outside of the womb
14. Homosexuality
15. Transexuals (the Archdiocese recently was petitioned for a

marriage license by a couple, one of whom had a sex change operation).

There was, in addition a reaffirmation of the 1976 decisions on abortion and homosexuality, as well as the 1974 decision on gambling. On the abortion issue, the Committee report stated: "Each day abortions have reached such an extent that it is unbelievable; although they are forbidden by the Church and are characterized as murder by the Church, it is murder of the conceived child before it sees the light of day. There are mothers who encourage their children to get abortions. A university last year announced to the co-eds that for those who become pregrant outside of marriage, it (the university) would gladly pay for the abortion."

On homosexuality, the Committee report stated: "Sexual misbehavior between men and women, between themselves and separately, has reached such a stage that the State is considering the enactment of a law so that men will cohabit with men, and women with women, despite the awful punishment which God inflicted on Sodom and Gomorrah, through which He reveals how strongly He forbids this sin. St. Paul also, in the first chapter of his epistle to the Romans (1 : 18-32), and the Spirit of the Lord from the time of the Old Testament condemns this sin as an act which surrenders man to the lowest corruption and debasement. Recently, in San Francisco, California, 250,000 young men and women homosexuals paraded in the main streets of the city, shouting demands that all rights which the citizens have be given to them. Cases have reached many courts and the state capitals in which homosexual teachers have demanded that they be allowed to teach the young in the public schools by law. Although Christ sanctifies the marriage of husband and wife and compares the Christian family to a small church, our morally fallen society has approached the total abolition of the Christian marriage with the cohabitation without civil or ecclesiastical marriage."

General interest, on the part of all the delegates is evident in the fact that the Congress also produced "a call to action for all churches and synagogues to join in an assault on the moral and social problems of modern society." A far cry from the 1960 Buffalo Congress, this militant statement stands as powerful evidence for the cumulative influence of Archbishop Iakovos on his church in the area of social concerns. Some paragraphs:

"Churches and synagogues should defend themselves by restructuring their spiritual and communal experience, and then assume the initiative by attacking: Atheism; Marxist Dialectics; Eudae-monism and hedonism; exploitation of religion by the various cults; and every movement and philosophy that violates and annihilates human rights and distorts the image of God which is in man."

"Much hard work of enlightenment and social action is required in the streets, in the ghettos, and wherever sin and shamelessness prevail." There might be difficulties and dangers in a frontal attack of this kind, but we should take the risk and assume the responsibility. A call to action brings rewards as well as dangers."

In addition, there were resolutions on the Year of the Child, on the City of Jerusalem as an Open City, on Peace and Disarmament, and an open letter to President Carter on the duty to express disagreement with the nation's foreign policy. This section concludes with a human rights statement as a fitting conclusion to all accumulation of evidence for social concern which began with the account of Archbishop Iakovos' participation in the Civil Rights March on Selma.

Statement on Human Rights by the 24th Biennial Clergy-Laity Congress of the Greek Orthodox Archdiocese of North and South America

Man has been created by God according to His own image and likeness, has been graced with a grace second only to that of the Angels themselves (Hebrews 2:7), has been adorned with a crown of glory and honor for the purpose of becoming a power of divine intent to be entrusted with ministering to those who are to inherit salvation (Hebrews 1:14), and finally, he has been redeemed by Christ at the price of His own life (I Cor. 7:23).

Our Church believes man to have a right of divine love, a love that derives from the supreme sacrifice of Christ Himself.

It also believes and teaches that the right of love that God has granted to men, man cannot deny to his fellow man.

These divinely inherent human rights include some such life situations and states of personal being as:

Freedom on all domains of human thought and expression, including political ideologies and life.

Intrinsic respect for the divine element in man that results in everyday experience in the state of self-respect and esteem by others.

Self-respect which in its turn is the result of social justice and recognition on the part of govenments of those elements in man that render him divine in the course of his finite experience and within his particular social setting.

Equal access for all to the right to vote, to be voted upon, and to assume a share of the govenment, of public experience and life.

Equal opportunity for all to become educated, to be offered employment, and to pursue in freedom, according to personal value and worth, their advancement in work and society; thereby, the abolishment of special privileges and rights usurped by those in economic, or any other type of power, at the expense of the weak, the poor, the semi-developed, the minorities, or the members of cultures other than themselves.

None of the above rights can be taken away from man. It is in support of this postulate, which issues from no less authority than that of the divine endowment of man, that this Clergy-Laity Congress deplores and protests the occasions when human rights are ignored or set aside for political expediency, however pressing this expediency may appear to be at times.

We further offer our unreserved support to our President, who has courageously and strongly demanded from the governments of all nations respect for human rights. And we urge him not to allow the sacred cause of human rights to be belittled, lessened in significance, or pushed aside by expediency or by those whose personal interests and lack of respect for the divine image in man dictate against human rights becoming the symbol and signal of a social order truly civilized and conducting its temporal experiences under God the Father.

25th CLERGY-LAITY CONGRESS. 1980, ATLANTA

Resolutions and statements, only, were officially issued by the 25th Clergy-Laity Congress. The report of the Social and Moral Issues Committee, together with fifteen position papers were referred to the Synod of Bishops for action and for final approval by the Ecumenical Patriarchate. Some of the resolutions and statements of more general interest and significance are the following:

Resolutions on Human and Religious Rights

WHEREAS, the 25th Biennial Congress of the Greek Orthodox Archdiocese of North and South America has convened in the great city of Atlanta, Georgia where AHEPA was founded by a courageous group of pioneer Greek Americans as an effective instrument in the never ending fight against bigotry and discrimination and "where the sermon for equal political and civil rights was heralded with the might of a lightening bolt by the martyred preacher, Martin Luther King," and

WHEREAS, the Orthodox Church believes and teaches that every human being, without exception, has received from God the inalienable right to freely practice his religious beliefs and tenets; and

WHEREAS, the United States of America has achieved its pre-eminent position among nations of the world through its respect for certain fundamental and divinely inherent human rights as exemplified by the Declaration of Independence and the Bill of Rights of the Federal Constitution; and:

WHEREAS, the United Nations Charter, the United Nations Declaration of Human Rights, the European Commission on Human Rights, the Helsinki Accord and other internationally accepted documents recognize the basic human rights of all people; and:

WHEREAS, human rights consist of those conditions of life that allow us fully to develop and use our human qualities of intelligence and conscience to their fullest extent, and to satisfy our spiritual, social and political needs, including freedom of expression, freedom from fear, harassment, intimidation and discrimination and freedom to participate in the functions of government and to have the guarantee of the equal protection of law; and:

WHEREAS, the policies and actions of certain governments of the world, whether through hypocritically subtle means or overt manifestations of systematic repression, have violated these basic human rights; and

WHEREAS, it is a shame and stigma for 20th century civilization that there are nations which, through insecurity resort to practices of the dark ages by holding hostages and that there are ruthless regimes which, by imposing indescribable suffering upon minorities living within their borders, force them to abandon their ancestral homes, which declare free citizens *persona non grata*, which forcibly prevent the free emigration of citizens seeking to leave, and which ostracize some as political exiles; and

WHEREAS, it is the moral and social responsibility and obligation of the free and democratic nations of this world to not only condemn and disavow such violations wherever they occur, but to take such affirmative steps as will restore realization of these inherent rights and a true respect thereof,

NOW, THEREFORE, BE IT RESOLVED by the 25th Clergy-Laity Congress of the Greek Orthodox Archdiocese of North and South America that we call upon totalitarian and oppressive regimes to restore respect for the rights and dignity of the individual and to insure the free and unhindered exercise of these vital rights by all citizens, regardless of racial or ethnic origin, or political or religious espousal; and:

BE IT FURTHER RESOLVED that we call upon all free and democratic governments of the world, and in particular the United States of America, to exercise their moral and political responsibilities for the preservation of human rights by adoption of clear, concise and consistent policies, both domestic and foreign, reflective of these fundamental human rights.

Resolution on Peace and Disarmament

WHEREAS, it is a fundamental Christian axiom that there is only one war which a Christian can fight: that "against the principalities, against the powers, against the rulers of the darkness of this world, against spiritual wickedness in high places" (Eph. 6, 12); and

WHEREAS, Christ blesses the peacemakers and calls them the children of God (Mt. 5, 9) and the Bible further exhorts us to "follow after those things which make for peace" (Rom. 14, 19); and

WHEREAS, as St. John Chrysostom has said, "It is certainly a greater and more wonderful work to change the minds of enemies bringing about a change of soul, than to kill them"; and

WHEREAS, peace is the goal and hope of mankind but peace to be real and lasting peace must be a peace based on mutal cooperation; not a blind trust,

NOW, THEREFORE, BE IT RESOLVED by the 25th Clergy-Laity Congress of the Greek Orthodox Archdioces of North and South America that we dedicate ourselves anew to the cause of peace and condemn and abhor all armed aggression including the invasion and continued occupation of Cyprus by Turkish armies; the invasion by Vietnam of its neighbors, the invasion of Afghanistan by Russia and the use of chemical warfare in said invasion; the presence and active participation of Cuban troops in African political turmoil; and

BE IT FURTHER RESOLVED that to prevent the ultimate destruction of mankind we call upon the leaders of all nations to exert every effort to de-escalate the arms race, and to work ceaselessly toward the goal of peace.

Statement on the Holy City of Jerusalem

"When He came near Jerusalem...the large crowd of his Disciples began to thank God and praise Him in loud voices..." (Luke 19:37)

WHEREAS, it is not coincidence of history that the City of Jerusalem is the most holy and sacred city in the World; and

WHEREAS, it was not mankind but God Himself, who in His Providential care, ordained that this city be the spiritual center for Jews, Christians and Moselms; and

WHEREAS, these three major faiths represent millions upon millions of the world's believers; and

WHEREAS, we Orthodox Christians have an overwhelming and awesome responsibility not only to preserve and to perpetuate our Churches, Holy Places and Shrines, but also to assure and guarantee the unhindered practice of Christian, Judaic and Mohammedan worship services; and

WHEREAS, Mr. Menachim Begin, the Prime Minister of Israel has announced the removal of his office to East Jerusalem asserting that Jerusalem is eternally a Jewish City,

NOW, THEREFORE, BE IT RESOLVED by the 25th Biennial Clergy-Laity Congress of the Greek Orthodox Archdiocese of North and South America that the Holy City of Jerusalem be declared a free city entrusted to the care not only of one tradition, or one faith, but to all three major faiths who collectively shall be charged with the awesome responsibility and task of preserving the free city concept, so that men and women of all religious faiths, who look upon Jerusalem as their Holy City, shall be free to live, travel and worship there and that the sanctity of that blessed and holy city be preserved.

Resolution on Third World Needs

WHEREAS, as brothers and sisters in Christ, we are commanded to become our brothers' helpers—"Whatever you did for one of least of those brothers of mine, you did for me" (Matthew 25:40); and

WHEREAS, we, as Orthodox Christians acknowledge that the earth is the dominion of the Lord, that all gifts and resources of the earth are from Him, "because the earth and its fullness belong to the Lord" and that we are the Stewards of the blessings and gifts which He has bestowed upon us; and

WHEREAS, there exist certain areas of our world, in particular the Third World, in which human suffering abounds in the form of poverty, hunger, inadequate shelters, lack of vital energy, and other deprivations of basic human needs; and

WHEREAS, all nations of the world should identify and use their best efforts to resolve such problems in order to assure stability and tranquility among the people of the world; and

WHEREAS, it is the moral and social responsibility of the more prosperous nations of the world to share their bounty with the deprived in an honest and sincere effort to reduce the disparity and to alleviate their poverty and suffering,

NOW, THEREFORE, BE IT RESOLVED by the 25th Biennial Congress of the Greek Orthodox Archdiocese of North and South America that we declare our deep concern for the tragedies which have befallen the people of the Third World, and offer our fervent prayers for them; and that this Congress calls upon the more prosperous nations of the world, Christian churches and other religious bodies and philanthropic organizations, to render every possible moral support and material assistance to the people of the Third World.

Resolution on Responsible Energy Sabbath

WHEREAS, according to Holy Scripture, God, is the source of all good things while we are merely stewards and users of His Divine Gifts, which we have at our disposal; and

WHEREAS, the Biblical tradition of the Sabbath is an ordination by God as a regular reminder that the earth is the Lord's and not ours to manipulate and deface at will; and

WHEREAS, the energy crisis grows more acute each day, forcing us to reorder our life-styles and priorities by calling upon us to conserve our nonrenewable energy sources, seek renewable energy sources, and share more equitably our resources; and

WHEREAS, an interfaith coalition of 40 churches, including the Greek Orthodox Archdiocese and five sponsoring agencies, including the National Council of Churches of Christ, have banded together to encourage and sponsor a nationwide yearlong Responsible Energy Sabbath, we, as sponsors, urge and encourage our parishes to participate in this project; and

BE IT FURTHER RESOLVED that we call for the designation of Sunday, October 19, 1980, as Responsible Energy Sabbath in every parish within the Archdiocese, with some appropriate acknowledgment of this event in each parish on that day.

Resolutions on the Family

WHEREAS, marriage was established by the Creator Himself, Who created Adam and Eve and blessed them and said: "Be fruitful and multiply, and fill the earth and subdue it" (Gen. 1:28); and

WHEREAS, according to the teaching of Holy Scripture, marriage is a Divine and sacred bond and the foundation of our universal human society; and

WHEREAS, God created male and female to complement each other and perpetuate the human race on earth, and to establish dominion where God's commandment and Will would be the ultimate law; and

WHEREAS, the year 1980 has been designated as "The Year of the Family,"

NOW, THEREFORE, BE IT RESOLVED by the 25th Clergy-Laity Congress of the Greek Orthodox Archdiocese of North and South America that we abhor "The New Moral Standards" which arise from a materialistic conception of life.

As is known, according to this materialistic understanding of life, the features of the Christian marriage, being mutual trust, love and spiritual unity, are ridiculed and grossly insulted. Couples are living together without guidance on the meaning of the sanctity of marriage and responsibility of parenthood, with the result that their children are becoming victims of their cruelty and exploitation by third parties.

According to the so-called 'New Morality,' there is a total departure from accepted moral standards and values. Today, attention is directed to a quest for quick thrills through drug abuse and alcoholism, both of which result in the destruction of the meaning of the family and family life, oftentimes leading to moral and physical death; and

BE IT FURTHER RESOLVED that the Church must and will guard against the undermining efforts of all adversaries of the Christian family including child abuse, the advocates of "the living together" style of life, the sad proponents of the "gay" movement and the abortionists; and

BE IT FURTHER RESOLVED that the Church must and will

always continue its efforts to preserve and safeguard the high moral standards of the Christian family without which a healthy and moral society cannot exist.

Statement on Religious Freedom

All people have the God-given right to be free from interference by government or others in 1) freely determining their faith by conscience, 2) freely associating and organizing with others for religious purposes; 3) expressing their religious beliefs in worship, teaching and practice; 4) and pursuing the implications of their beliefs in the social and political community.

Today, in all parts of the world, there are forces that attempt to repress these religious rights and, indeed to eliminate all religious faith. The effort to repress rights and faith betrays a basic disdain for the godly and civic virtues of justice, tolerance, compassion and charity. The contempt for man leads to the contempt for God and faith.

We believe we must be ever-vigilant in the struggle of peoples for religious freedom. We must be ready to cooperate with all those who sincerely work for the dignity and religious rights of mankind. We who freely exercise our Orthodoxy must be ready to assist those persecuted for their beliefs.

We give special attention at this Congress to the growing persecution of Orthodox Christians because of their identity, faith and religious practice, and are today especially concerned over the arrest for religious reasons and unjust detainment of our brothers and sisters in the Soviet Union.

We are especially inspired by, and appreciative of, the endorsement, leadership, and financial assistance provided by His Eminence Archbishop Iakovos to the new Freedom and Faith Foundation. We urge Greek Orthodox Christians throughout the Archdiocese to work with their parishes and to join hands with other Christians of their communities to form local groups of this Foundation so that united we might be able to better help guarantee the religious rights of believers of all traditions.

Statement on Moral and Social Issues

The Orthodox Church, in its care for the spiritual, the moral and the social welfare of its members throughout the world appeals to the reason and conscience of all to reconsider their attitude towards all problems of personal and community concern and look, not for easy solutions which legalize the illegal, but rather for solutions in the light of Christ's teachings and Christian doctrine and to recognize the validity of the Christian axioms that God is the Way, the Truth and the Life, and to Whom we raise our souls and hands, and that only truth to God and to one another can lead us to true freedom from fear and insecurity and to a pragmatic evaluation of the nature of the solutions we pursue.

It is the belief of this Clergy-Laity Congress that Christians of today are called upon to "transform all that is plastic and temporal in our society into vital, exuberant and renewing moral values and concerns"; and further, that Christians must learn to act positively and responsibly convince themselves that they, and they alone, can correct the ills of our times such as wastefulness, violence, the acceptance of crime as a norm of society, injustice and the shameless justification of the unjust, sexual abuse, child-crime, poverty, hunger, terror, collapse of moral values, and exploitation in the ranks of our society.

Only if we are armed with impenetrable Christian concepts and beliefs, galvanizing at the same time all of the power of our being and our faith, will we be able to respond to the spiritual and moral crises of our time.

Statement on Morality in International Relations

The 25th Clergy-Laity Congress expresses its painful concern at the contradictory and self-serving polity and often hypocritical policies of the governments of the World Powers as all too frequently manifested in their actions and pronouncements.

We decry the blatant disrespect and shameful abuse of the hallowed words – "democracy," "peace," and "justice" by totalitarian and oppressive regimes throughout the world in their application to situations and conditions which are the direct opposite to the true meaning of these words.

We disapprove of governmental policies and actions which violate the unalienable rights of all men to freedom and human dignity.

We are disillusioned and dismayed at the selective and hypocritical manner in which armed aggression and the violation of human rights by some nations are condemned, while similar acts by others are either ignored, or even worse, shamelessly justified.

We express our indignation at the gross insensitivity of the so-called great or super powers of the world towards small and defenseless nations and racial minorities of the world, and the cynical manner in which they are used or abused by these powers to further what they believe to be their interests or the interests of their allies. The Blacks in South Afrrica; the Thais and Tibetans; the Georgians, Ukranians, Latvians, Esthonians and Lithuanians in the Soviet Union, the Afghans and the Kurds in both Iran and Turkey; the Greek Cypriots in Cyprus, the Greeks in Northern Epirus, the Armenian and Greek minorities in Turkey—all these and many others are not included among the concerns of these powers unless they can serve as useful and valuable pawns in their political chessgame.

Marriage and the Family

Preface

The Sanctity of the Family Institution (The Household Assembly)

Writers of the history of religion say that the unity of two persons of the opposite sex in primitive societies always followed religious precepts and stipulations.

If these stipulations and solemnities were not carried out within a religious context, then the unity of two persons of the opposite sex was considered to be a violation of the sacred institution and an illegal act having destructive consequences on the future of the human race.

The Holy Bible. According to the Holy Bible, marriage was established by God with the joining of Adam and Eve to live as husband and wife. God blessed the first couple and charged them to be fruitful and multiply and fill the earth (Gen. 1:27,28; Tob.8:6).

According to God's precepts, marriage is a sacred institution. The natural institution becomes sacred with God's blessings. Wherever a relationship between man and woman exists, as described above, it also means that there is a relationship between God and the beloved couple (Isaiah 54:6).

During the long period from the fall of man until the coming of Christ, marriage devolved into polygamy. Nevertheless, Christ reestablished monogamy and proclaimed the vital importance of the Christian marriage. This is described in the New Testament, when the Lord:

a) Spoke against adultery and divorce (Matt. 5:28-37).

b) Replied to the Pharisees who asked him about a man being allowed to divorce his wife for whatever reason (Matt. 19:3-12; Mark 10:1-2; and Luke 16:18).

c) Spoke to the Saducees who denied the Resurrection and tried to put him into a difficult position with their question concerning the woman who married seven brothers in succession and her relationship to the seven brothers in the Kingdom of Heaven (Matt. 22:23-33).

On the basis of the aforementioned, it is obvious that Christ gave sanctity to marriage and that the spiritual unity of two persons contributes significantly to the fulfillment of man's life on earth.

Every marriage is a matter that involves God and the couple who are entering marriage. The Lord even honored marriage with a miracle and, being truly the Son of God, Who is of one essence with the Father, He declared, "Those whom God has joined together, let no man separate" (Matt. 19:6).

St. Paul the Apostle says, "Marriage is honorable in all, and the bed undefiled" (Heb. 13:4). He called marriage a sacrament: "This is a great mystery, but I speak concerning Christ and the Church" (Eph. 5:32).

Marriage, arising from an agreement between a man and a woman, is certified and blessed by the Church. The fruits of a marriage are unswerving love, spiritual unity, happiness and the birth of children. Every Orthodox family is a small church resembling the congregation of the early Christians.

Faith, mutual trust, love and spiritual unity, which strengthens whatever time has eroded, must prevail in the family. Spiritual unity makes the family a "Church in the house" (household Church). Every Greek Orthodox family must be a house of the Lord, striving toward the same goals and living the very life of the Church.

The Inviolability of the Family Insitution and the Dangers it Faces

The Orthodox Christian couple has a common faith and lifestyle, and they worship the Lord together in spirit and truth. They worship unitedly in the Church and together receive Holy Communion.

However, when the couple does not fulfill their religious responsibilities, or when the spirit of the world meddles in the life of the couple, then the possibility increases that their marriage be dissolved.

In today's world, because of pressures and influence of materialism, modernism and daily distractions, the family is undergoing increasing difficulties, causing more and more marriages to end in divorce. Historically, divorce was always associated with a laxness of morals. We find reference to divorces in the age of Rome and the time of the Old Testament (Deut. 24:1).

Jesus, the Supreme and eternal Lawmaker, wanted to put an

end to the easy way of obtaining divorce. Only the death of one of the couple, or the moral death (adultery) of one of the two, gives freedom to the other party to enter into a second marriage.

The Christian family today is very lax in its regard for the permanency of marriage. People seek divorce today, not only because of adultery or unfaithfulness, but even because they feel they are not financially secure. Husbands and wives are abandoning one another. They are squandering their money gambling or drinking. They are becoming unable to continue handling their responsibilities. After living together for many years, they discover that they are no longer compatible, or that they are putting each other through mental anguish and abuse.

However, the real cause of divorce is that faith, moral integrity and respect for each other, all of which are given from God (Gen. 1: 26) no longer exist in their relationship.

It happens so often in our day; quick marriage and quick divorce; marriage out of necessity to give a child a name; or freedom for a couple to live together without the sanctity of marriage or the responsibility of motherhood. This is compounded in our time by the greater attention that is being given to the hedonisitc way of life—the quest for quick thrills which is often accompanied by drug abuse and poses real danger of spiritual and physical death.

On the other hand, living conditions are becoming more difficult every day. The cost of living is increasing constantly. Life's demands are becoming more unbearable every day. People prefer to live "free" without sharing the responsibilities of supporting children and facing the daily increasing financial hardships.

According to information disclosed in a conference which took place in the White House early in 1980 regarding the "Family," Jo Ann Gasper from McLean, Virginia, said: "Two unmarried, unrelated people are not a family. How true! The reduction in the number of marriages and births is the result of unmarried people living together. This is a principal cause in the dissolution of the family."

What is becoming evident through statistics recorded in the Archdiocese's registry books is that Orthodox Christians are beginning to live in a manner that does not conform to the Faith. Husbands are ceasing to love their wives, and wives are not showing respect to themselves or their husbands.

The so-called "New Moral Standard," which is gaining prevalence, gives license to everything which undermines the Christian family life. However, the Church will always continue its efforts to preserve and safeguard the high moral standards of the Christian family because they guarantee a healthy, moral society.

The Christian family will always be upheld by the Church as a sacred institution, and those who enter an Orthodox Christian marriage will always be considered members of the Body of Christ and the most basic foundation of human society.

The Christian family must be preserved as an ideal within the framework of Christianity's spiritual and moral principles because "This is the will of God in Christ Jesus towards us" (Thess. 5:18).

We truly need to arise from the deep slumber of a materialistic conception of life. We need a true spiritual and moral revolution and a strong defense against the current materialistic outlooks on life. We also need to continue our effort to rediscover ourselves as creatures of God. These efforts will, with the grace and help of God, help us achieve greater self-discipline and make us more responsible in our commitment to build a better society under God and in accordance with His Will and precepts.

This chapter has sought to do no more than provide the reader with otherwise difficult to locate texts of the social concerns of the Greek Orthodox Archdiocese during this period for further study, as a service to the discipline of Orthodox Christian ethics and theological scholarship in general.

In the process, the basic thesis of this book seems to be overwhelmingly proven. I wish to conclude with what seems to be a summary statement from the Keynote Address to the 24th Clergy-Laity Congress. It seems to describe in short what the evidence demonstrates.

We may not be as numerous or as resourceful as other Christians. Nevertheless, we can certainly promote and elevate Orthodoxy if we become more active and truly involved in the ecumenical effort of the Church, i. e., to bring about a better and more just and humane order in the world. It is high time that we disengage ourselves from the countless and tiring, petty preoccupations and engage ourselves in a concerted effort in order to recapture, in a meaningful way, both the unity and the mission of Orthodoxy in the present-day world.

Chapter Six

NO CONCLUSIONS—MANY QUESTIONS

The purpose of this study has been, primarily, to gather together, in a convenient and accessible place, the evidence and sources regarding the existence of social concern in the Greek Orthodox Archdiocese of North and South America. It is hoped that students of social ethics, as well as clergy and lay persons, will avail themselves of the accumulated material so as to continue to develop social concern in the Orthodox Church in the decades to come. It is also hoped that the material compiled here will serve to influence commonly held perceptions about the Orthodox Church's views and attitudes on social concern in general and specific issues in particular.

As a consequence, no general conclusion, synthesis or theological analysis was intended to be included in this study. It is hoped by the author that all that was intended, has been accomplished: the presentation of evidence. Perhaps a future study can do the deeper analysis which may provide guiding insights for the future. Certainly, it is anticipated that students of Orthodox Christian ethics will wish to give thoughtful attention and reflection to the evidence gathered in this volume, whether these be seminarians, theologians, parish priests, individual bishops, Clergy-Laity Congresses, or synods of the Church.

In spite of this stated restriction on the purpose of this study, it might not be inappropriate to assess some immediate *impressions* (as distinguished from *conclusions*) arrived at from a careful theological and statistical analysis of the evidence.

The following is only a set of impressions and reflections from the accumulated material, and certainly subject to more careful study and analysis.

The *results of the documentation* seem to provide more material than was originally expected. The original assumption when the study was undertaken was that there would, in fact, be only a minimal amount of statements in the encyclicals evincing social concern; next to nothing in the keynote addresses; and only a small range of concerns in the Moral and Social Concerns Committees of the Clergy-Laity Congresses.[1] Though one ought not read too much into, or over-emphasize the results of this study, it is, in fact, rather surprising to find as much evidence for social concern as was found.

This is particularly true in the light of the widely-held view, both within and outside the Orthodox Church, that Eastern Orthodox Christianity does not concern itself with social issues, and even more strongly, may not concern itself with public morality because of an inherent theological reason. Both the historical overview and the evidence of the recent past years of the Greek Orthodox Archdiocese tend to argue against that view.

The *emerging pattern* seems to be a cautious, careful and conservative resumption of the older traditions of social concern in Eastern Christianity. The combination of circumstances in the Greek Orthodox Archdiocese, not to mention the leading of God's Holy Spirit, seems to have provided the Church with the appropriate "moment," a spiritual *kairos*, for Orthodox Christianity to begin to see, once again, the implications of its beliefs on the social fabric of the world in which it lives. Not the least of these "circumstances" is a particularly inspired and visionary hierarch, Archbishop Iakovos, who has assumed a prophetic role regarding social concern. Often, it must have seemed in truth a "voice crying in the wilderness," with little or no response or resonance in the body of the Church. For some, these appeals had no more than the sound of empty public relations statements designed "for external consumption only." In some cases, such as the Archbishop's participation in the Selma march and demonstration, it was the cause of angry denunciation. But the progression from Encyclicals to Keynote addresses to social and moral issues committees which we have seen implies some significant pastoral leadership which cannot be dismissed lightly, especially in the light of the previous history of the Archdiocese.

Another important influence, it would seem, is the impact on the Orthodox of the radically new climate of an environment of Church-State relations as compared to the previous history of the Orthodox. The history of the Greek Orthodox Church's relationship to the public sphere showed two rather long periods which were diametrically opposed to each other. The Byzantine period was a time of "symphonia," a period where ideally, at least, two independent agencies—the State and the Church—worked in harmony together for the well-being of a common body which was concurrently composed of citizens of the Empire and members of the same Church.[2] The period of "Tourkokratia," from 1453 (and earlier for most of the Empire) to 1829 was the occasion for a sharp division of the Church from the dominant power and a "second-class" status. Orthodox presence in the American and

Western European milieu of friendly and supportive separation of Church and State is new. It may be seen as a synthesis of the previous thesis (Byzantine "Symphonia") and antithesis (Tourkokratic antagonistic separatism), calling forth a rediscovery of ancient attitudes and values in a new format. Thus, the idea will precede actual action. It would seem that there are not many to be found to actively reject the principle of Orthodox Christian social concern and — ultimately — involvement in appropriate ways.

A further influence is to be found in the general spirit of Orthodox involvement in the Ecumenical movement. It is clear that, deliberately or not, this involvement has challenged the Orthodox to come to terms in one way or another with issues of social concern. Thus, one student of the subject notes:

> Without delving into the finer points of Orthodox ecumenical relations, one knows that by participating in the World Council of Churches alone, Orthodoxy expresses a fundamental concern for social improvement and involvement. Articulating its importance for the faith, Father Robert Stephanopoulos notes the W.C.C.'s value in the fact that "it places mission and service at the center of the church's life." He comments, "...active cooperation in the agonizing spheres of human problems, charitable encounters with one another, openness to the promptings of the Spirit—all these are the means of true ecumenism which seeks to lead separated Christians out of their mutual hostility, isolation and fragmentation into convergence, reintegration and reunion."[3]

If this were, indeed, the only influence upon the Greek Orthodox Church's revival of social concern, the charge that it represents a "protestantization" of Greek Orthodoxy would be hard to refute. But, as we have seen in the first chapter of this study, such is not the case at all. To deny, however, the catalytic influence of the WCC and ecumenism in this area would be both erroneous and ungracious.

Perhaps there are other factors as well. Whatever the case, Edward Duff's judgment about Orthodox social concern cannot be held to be true anymore. Writing before 1956, he said:

> Orthodox groups...seem to have no specific contribution to make the effort to analyze and resolve the peril for all mankind which is without precedent in the whole of human history.[4]

The evidence presented in this study seems to dispute this. His judgment, however, is still partially true regarding careful theological analysis and exposition of an Orthodox social ethic. He said:

> The Orthodox Churches have not seriously, nor systematically, concerned themselves with social or political questions as problems for the Christian mind as well as tasks for Christian charity.[5]

The extensive bibliographies included in the footnotes of the first chapter of this study have been presented to show that there has not been an absence of concern for social issues among the Greek Orthodox. But it is true that only now are there beginning attempts to develop a clear and articulate social ethic. Whether, by the nature of Orthodox theology itself, such an ethic can or ought to be systematic in the western sense, is doubtful. Serious? Yes. Systematic?; Perhaps not. It should be noted, for instance, that one of the ten topics for discussion at the forthcoming Great and Holy Council of the Orthodox Church deals with issues of social concern.

Such a reflection leads to an assessment of *problems* arising from this study. By its very nature, the evidence presented here raises a number of questions for the reader and those interested in the development of social concern in the Orthodox Church.

Thus, one cannot help but wonder if the personal impact of Archbishop Iakovos, which seems to have been crucial in this impetus in the development of social concern, will outlive his hieratical service in the future. The evidence seems to point both ways. Certainly, in the face of several suggestions on his part pointing to his retirement, both the interests of the hierarch in general as well as the concerns of his successor will play a significant role.

Criticism has been made of the hesitancy of the Church to assume an active role in social concerns areas. John Chirban has put it well: "The sermonic, didactic 'decisions' of the Clergy-Laity Congresses have done little to bring action on the subjects of war, racism, sexual perversion and the like. What is needed is programming to stir awareness...(we are) called to put less time to rhetoric and respond to social mission realistically."[6] Perhaps it is only a question of time for the "didactic" approach to bear fruit in action. But it certainly is possible for the social concern expressed in the Clergy-Laity Congresses to be taken as an adequate "tip of the hat," to these issues, requiring from the Church nothing more. This certainly would not be justified, but the danger is there. The question is, what is being done to help the pronouncements become action?

A related question is, "who will do it?" Can the future development of the social and moral implications of the Orthodox faith be entrusted to one group within the Church? Is it the province of the hierarchy or the priests? Can it ever develop as a church force without the laity? Ought it be the sole province of an official office? Ought there to be nonofficial, but clearly Orthodox agencies working in this area? Is a separate publication needed? Probably a correct response will incorporate all these aspects. Extremely important, however, as indicated above, is the role of the hierarchy; their stance will provide the climate.

The question of methodology is now quite important. At heart, and in the first instance, is study and theological reflection. The Clergy-Laity Congresses of 1978 and 1980 seem to have sensed this and asked for studies on specific questions. But for these to take place, careful preliminary and foundational questions have to be asked with the pragmatic goals in mind. Here is where theological investigation is important. But it is clear from the fact of Orthodox ecclesiology that the theologian's desk can only initiate the process. The mind of the Church—in so much as it reflects the faith and the Christian ethos—expressed by the people, the clergy and the hierarchy is even more important. There seems to be a need to devise a method by which issues of social concern in the Church can be addressed thoroughly, yet without undue delay. Both the articulation of views and organization for action need such methodological clarification.

The Clergy-Laity Congresses are biennial affairs and though there is, clearly, representation from the parish level, the issue of dissemination to the diocesan and parish level is important. At heart, it is only a part of the total educational effort of the Church. How much of the church's effort, in the nurture of the Christian life, focuses on moral issues which transcend private ethics? A study of the curricular material prepared for use in church schools, the contents of church publications, sermons, lectures, camp curricula, and adult classes, would, I am sure, provide very little evidence for concern with social issues. If concern on these levels is not felt, then, to be sure, there will be little or no movement toward the implementation of Orthodox ethics in the public sphere.

Yet, it would seem that this is not a situation restricted to the area of social concerns. How does the development of a social conscience relate to the effort to develop spiritual renewal and mission? Are these "out reach" areas unrelated? It would seem to me that resistance to any one of the three usually means resistance to the others, and conversely, those for whom spiritual growth becomes important will also find mission outreach and social concern important as well. The Orthodox Consultation held in Etchmiadzine, in 1975, on the topic "Confessing Christ through the Liturgical Life of the Church," stated that "the liturgy must not be limited to the celebration in the Church, but has to be continued in the life of the faithful in all dimensions of life."[8] Fr. Ion Bria draws the spiritual aspects of liturgy to their earthly implications:

> The liturgical life has to nourish the Christian life not only in its private sphere, but also in its public and political realm. One cannot separate the true Christian identity from the personal sanctification and love and service to man (1 Peter 14-15). There is an increasing concern today about the ethical implications of the faith, in terms of life style, social ethic and human behavior. What is the *ethos* of the Church which claims to be the sign of the Kingdom? What is the "spirituality" which is proposed and determined in spreading the Gospel and celebrating the Liturgy today? How is the liturgical vision which is related to the Kingdom, as power of the age to come, as the beginning of the future life which is infused in the present life (John 3:5, 6:33), becoming a social reality? What does sanctification or *theosis* mean in terms of ecology and human rights?[9]

Such are these and many more questions raised by this study. The affirmations raise more questions, so without doubt what has preceded these pages cannot be seen as anything other than a record of a new beginning. It is founded in a spiritual reality which needs to be understood theologically, articulated ecclesially, and made a part of the consciousness of the Church once again. It needs to be perceived as an outreaching imperative of Christian love for all who call Christ Lord and it must be put into organized and personal practice. Thus, the title of this final section is the only possible result of the study which has led us to this point—a point which now looks forward to the future. As far as Orthodox social concerns are concerned, there is no conclusion but there are many questions.

NOTES

1. A brief survey of some of the material was published in 1974 by John Chirban in "Orthodoxy's Social Character as Implemented in the Greek Orthodox Archdiocese of North and South America," EKPHRASIS, 2, no. 2 (1974), pp. 17-34.

2. Constantinos D. Mouratides, *Scheseis Ekklesias kai politeias* (Athens, 1965).

3. Chirban, *EKPHRASIS*, p. 31. Quotations from Robert Stephanopoulos "Reflections on Orthodox Ecumenical Directions After Uppsala," *Journal of Ecumenical Studies*, 9 (1972), pp. 301-317.

4. Edward Duff, *The Social Teaching of the World Council of Churches* London, 1956), p. 128.

5. *Ibid.*, p. 129.

6. *Ibid.*, pp. 33-34. See also Exetastes, *Contemporary Issues: Orthodox Christian Perspectives* (New York, 1976), pp. 72-75 for an assessment or social concern hesitancy on the part of the membership of the 1974 Clergy-Laity Congress as regards action.

7. For example, see "The *liturgy* after the *Liturgy*," in Ion Bria, *Martyria and Mission: The Witness of the Orthodox Churches Today*, ed. Ion Bria (Geneva, 1980), pp. 66-74.

8. "The Etchmiaadzine Report," *International Review of Mission*, 64, 256 (1975), pp. 417-21.

9. Bria, *Martyria and Mission*, p. 70; emphasis added.

INDEX